Crossway Bible Guide

Series Editors: Ian Coffey (NT), Stephen Gaukroger (OT)
New Testament Editor: Stephen Motyer

Also in this series

Exodus: Stephen Dray
Joshua: Charles Price
Ezra and Nehemiah: Dave Cave
Acts: Stephen Gaukroger
1 Peter: Andrew Whitman

Dedicated to
the church family at MBC,
with gratitude.

Philippians: Crossway Bible Guide
Free to be God's People

Ian Coffey

Crossway Books
Nottingham

ISBN 1-85684-085-9

Unless otherwise stated, Scripture quotations in this publication are
from the Holy Bible, New International Version. Copyright © 1973,
1978, 1984 International Bible Society. Published in Great Britain by
Hodder & Stoughton Ltd.

Typeset by Saxon Graphics Ltd, Derby.
Printed in Great Britain for Crossway Books, Norton Street,
Nottingham NG7 3HR, by Cox & Wyman Ltd, Reading, Berkshire.

Contents

Crossway Bible Guides

Series Editors' Introduction

Today, the groups of people who meet together to study the Bible appear to be a booming leisure-time activity in many parts of the world. In the United Kingdom alone, over one million people each week meet in home Bible-study groups.

This series has been designed to help such groups and, in particular, those who lead them. We are also aware of the needs of those who preach and teach to larger groups as well as the hard-pressed student, all of whom often look for a commentary that gives a concise summary and lively application of a particular passage. We have tried to keep three clear aims in our sights:

1 To explain and apply the message of the Bible in non-technical language.
2 To encourage discussion, prayer and action on what the Bible teaches.
3 To enlist authors who are in the business of teaching the Bible to others and are doing it well.

All of us engaged in the project believe that the Bible is the Word of God – given to us in order that people might discover Him and His purposes for our lives. We believe that the 66 books which go to make up the Bible, although written by different people, in different places, at different times, through different circumstances, have a single unifying theme: that theme is Salvation.

All of us hope that the books in this series will help people get a grip on the message of the Bible. But most important of all, we pray that the Bible will get a grip on you as a result!

Ian Coffey
Stephen Gaukroger
Series Editors

Note to readers

In our Bible Guides we have developed special symbols to make things easier to follow. Every passage therefore has an opening section which is

the passage in a nutshell

The main section is the one that *makes sense of the passage.*
This is marked with a blackboard.

Questions: Every passage also has special questions for group and personal study in a box after the main section. Some questions are addressed to us as individuals, some speak to us as members of our church or home group, while others concern us as members of God's people worldwide.

Some passages, however, require an extra amount of explanation, and we have put these sections into two categories. The first kind gives additional background material that helps us to understand something complex. For example, if we study the Gospels, it helps us to know who the Pharisees were, so that we can see more easily why they related to Jesus in the way they did. These technical sections are marked with an open book.

Finally, some passages have important doctrines contained in them, which we need to study in more depth if we are to grow as Christians. Special sections that explain them to us in greater detail are marked with a mortar board.

How to use this book

This book has been written on the assumption that it will be used in one of three ways:

● for individuals using it as an aid to personal study
● for groups wishing to use it as a study guide to Philippians
● for those preparing to teach others.

The following guidelines will help you to get the most from the material.

Personal study

One of the best methods of Bible study is to read the text through carefully several times possibly using different versions or translations. Having reflected on the material it is a good discipline to write down your own thoughts before doing anything else. At this stage the introduction of other books can be useful. If you are using this book as your main study resource, then read through the relevant sections carefully, turning up the Bible references that are mentioned. The questions at the end of each chapter are specifically designed to help you to apply the passage to your own situation. You may find it helpful to write your answers to the questions in your notes.

It is a good habit to conclude with prayer, bringing before God the things you have learned. If you follow the chapters of this book as a guide for studying Philippians you will find it divides up into twenty-seven separate studies of manageable length.

Group study

There are two choices:

a. You can take the ten main sections as a weekly study.
b. You can opt for the twenty-seven separate chapters as a weekly study.

Members of the group should follow the guidelines set out above for *Personal Study*. It is recommended that your own notes should contain:

a. Questions or comments on verses that you wish to discuss with the whole group.
b. Answers to the questions at the end of each section.

The format of your group time will depend on your leader, but it is suggested that the answers to the questions at the end of each section form a starting point for your discussions.

Teaching aid

If you are using this book as an aid to teaching others it may be helpful for you to note that the material has been divided into ten sections as follows:

Partners together	1:1–11
How to live and how to die	1:12–26
Standing firm	1:27–30
Learning to serve	2:1–11
How to be holy	2:12–18
Godly leadership	2:19–30
What are you trusting in?	3:1–11
Pressing on	3:12–4:1
How to survive in a local church	4:2–9
Caring and sharing	4:10–23

The sections provide a division of the material in Philippians in a way that breaks up the text without destroying the flow of teaching. Each section contains chapters (never more than three per section) which deal with the key points in the text. If the above sections are used it provides a ten week study course. The questions at the end of each chapter can easily be adapted for group use as appropriate.

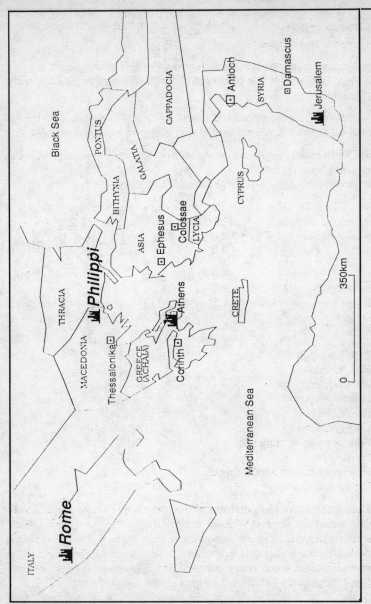

Map 1:   Philippi in the time of Paul
Michael Bradshaw

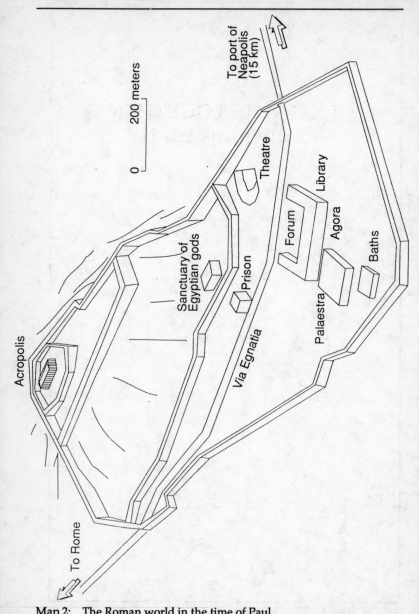

Map 2:   The Roman world in the time of Paul
Michael Bradshaw

PARTNERS TOGETHER
Philippians 1:1–11

1

Philippians 1:1–2

Introduction

Paul begins his thank you letter with an introduction which includes the Lord Jesus Christ at every point.

Every society has rules for polite behaviour – these extend to ordinary activities such as letter writing. Almost without thinking we start a letter 'Dear ...' and at the end sign ourselves off in an appropriate way.

The world in which the New Testament was written had rules of good behaviour too. The standard opening for any letter would be:

From   with the name of the person writing the letter
To   the name of the person who will receive it
Greeting   an opening phrase to fit the occasion.

Paul is writing this letter from prison (or possibly under conditions of house arrest) to the congregation of Christians in the city of Philippi. He follows polite custom as he begins his letter but uses words and phrases that are rich in meaning for Christians. Each of the three standard parts of the opening letter include the Lord Jesus Christ.

He starts with the '**From**'; including his colleague *Timothy*, his highly valued right-hand man (see 2:19 and *What do we know about Timothy?* pp73–74). He describes himself and Timothy as 'servants' – the actual word means 'slaves'. In New Testament times, a slave had no rights and belonged completely to his or her owner. Paul is expressing the fact that he and Timothy are sold out to the ownership of Jesus Christ.

Paul uses the same description in two of his other letters (Rom. 1:1 and Tit. 1:1) and is keen to point out that he is first and foremost a slave of Christ. This is particularly important for the Philippians as later in his letter Paul goes on to encourage them to be more humble in their dealings with each other (2:1–11). He starts by practising what he will soon be preaching.

Paul moves to the 'To' part of his introduction: 'To all the saints in Christ Jesus at Philippi'. Having described himself as a slave he calls the Christians at Philippi saints. We could have expected Paul – a powerful Christian leader – to have put it the other way round! The word *saint* is the word used more than any other in the New Testament to describe a follower of Jesus – occurring over sixty times. Surprisingly by comparison, the word *Christian* appears only three times. The word translated *saint* can also mean *holy* and this gives an important clue to its meaning. Forget the idea that saints are a select handful of spiritual superheroes consigned to stained-glass window fame. In the New Testament all true followers of Jesus are described as saints – people set apart by God and called to live differently.

Paul singles out from the congregation two groups of people described as 'overseers and deacons'. (The word for overseer has sometimes been translated *bishop* and the word for deacon as *minister*.) Some people like to think that the New Testament provides us with a perfect blueprint of how to run the Church but what we actually have is more of a sketch plan. That is why Christians from different denominations can point to the Bible to justify their way of doing things as being the right way!

There seems to have been a degree of flexibility in how congregations were organized in the days of the Early Church, although Paul as an apostle (messenger) of the Lord Jesus, appointed leaders wherever new congregations were planted (see Acts 14:23) and gave clear teaching about the character qualifications for such people (see 1 Tim. 3:1–13). These leaders had the task of overseeing and caring for the believers. Why does Paul single out the leadership at Philippi in a way which is unique in his writings? It could be that as this is an official thank you note for a gift of money received from the congregation (see 4:18) Paul feels he should acknowledge those who have possibly arranged the special collection. It also tells us something about the close relationship between the apostle and the church at Philippi, particularly its leadership team who have worked with him in the past (see 4:3).

The third part of a standard letter was the 'Greeting'. Paul makes sure this is not an empty gesture or a general 'all the best'. He wants his friends at Philippi to receive two gifts: 'Grace and peace to you from

God the Father and the Lord Jesus Christ' (verse 2). These two gifts are received when we start to follow Christ and are constantly needed as we continue as disciples. *Grace* is the basis on which God deals with us. It is his undeserved love which reaches us with the offer of forgiveness and a fresh start through the death of Jesus on our behalf (Eph. 1:7). *Peace* is a deep inner rest that comes when we are living in a right relationship with God and others (Rom. 5:1). Both gifts come from God the Father and his Son, Jesus.

Paul turns the formal opening of the letter to bring the Lord Jesus Christ into every phrase. He is the one who has made such a difference for Paul and his friends at Philippi.

Questions

1. *What does the phrase 'slave of Christ' convey to you? Would you use it to describe to someone else what it means to be a Christian?*

2. *What does it mean in the New Testament sense to be a 'saint'? How should a Christian behave in the light of such a description?*

3. *Make a note of people you know personally who need God's grace and peace and pray for them by name.*

Philippi – The city and its history

Philippi was the first major centre in Europe that Paul visited and where he established a church. The Philippian believers were the first European church, being situated, in modern day geography, in the north-eastern corner of Greece (see map 2).

On the site of the city originally there was a village named Krenides ('Springs'). It was taken over by Greek settlers some 360 years before the birth of Jesus Christ.

A king named Philip II of Macedonia (whose main claim to fame was that he was the father of Alexander the Great) formally established the city in 356 BC and gave it his own name – Philippi.

He made it a strategic military centre and the city walls built at this time can still be seen today. It commanded the main road from Europe to Asia and was near to gold and silver mines that produced much wealth for Philip.

When the Romans conquered the area of Macedonia, Philippi became a key city for administration. An important battle was fought at

Philippi in 42 BC when Mark Anthony and Octavian defeated the Roman Republican forces of Brutus and Cassius – the men who had assassinated Julius Caesar. This decided the future direction of the whole Roman Empire.

Not long afterwards, Philippi was awarded the highest possible honour in being made a Roman colony. The privileges attached to this distinction were great. Citizens of Philippi became citizens of Rome. They wore Roman clothes, spoke the Roman language, observed Roman customs. It was reflected in the architecture of the city as Philippi was modelled on Rome with streets and buildings laid out as copies. Even the coins carried Roman inscriptions. Their constitution and legal structures were modelled on Roman Law.

There was great pride in this privilege. This is illustrated by the words of the charge laid against Paul and Silas when they first visited Philippi:

> These men are Jews and are throwing our city into an uproar by advocating customs unlawful for us Romans to accept or practise (Acts 16:20–21).

Paul uses this sense of pride in the city's status as a telling illustration in his letter. He reminds the Philippian Christians 'but our citizenship is in heaven' (see 3:20). The inference was clear, they were to carry an even greater sense of pride and dignity that they belonged as citizens of the Kingdom of Heaven.

2

Philippians 1:3–8

Thank God!

Paul thanks God for the partnership of the Christians at Philippi and reveals his deep affection for them.

Paul had a close relationship with the Christian believers in Philippi and is able to thank God for their friendship (verse 3). He tells them that they are on his prayer list (verse 4). His praying for them is constant – 'in all my prayers', comprehensive – 'for all of you' and cheerful – 'I always pray with joy'. It appears that Paul prayed for the congregation, individual by individual, on a regular basis and this was a joyful experience for him. His relationship with local churches was not always sweetness and light so what gave him such a positive attitude towards the Philippians?

First, he had happy memories of the way they first received the message about Jesus (see Acts 16:11–40). It had been a costly venture with Paul and his fellow preacher Silas being publicly whipped and thrown into prison. But Paul had no regrets as quite a few people found faith and became vibrant Christians. It had cost Paul a great deal to see the church at Philippi come to birth, little wonder he felt such a strong attachment to the people there.

Second, he was glad that they had stuck with him over the eleven or twelve years that had passed since the church was planted. He describes this as their 'partnership in the gospel' (verse 5) and uses the famous New Testament word often translated *fellowship*. For the Philippians this meant more than a limp handshake and a cup of tea (which is the level to which some Christians today have relegated the word) but practical partnership. They had sent one of their leaders with a financial gift to Paul and this was not the first time they had demonstrated their costly care for him (4:10, 14–15). Such kindness had touched Paul's heart.

Third, Paul was glad about the truth that God always finishes what he starts. God had begun to do good things in their lives and this work would carry on until the Lord Jesus returned (verse 6). In spite of his own difficult circumstances, Paul was optimistic and thankful to God for his Philippian partners.

He goes on to explain how deeply he feels this attachment to them (verse 7) yet he acknowledges this is a result of the love of Christ at work in him (verse 8). This is an important point for us to note when we find it hard to get along with fellow-Christians. We sometimes struggle to produce a loving feeling from within ourselves, only to end up feeling condemned that we find some people difficult to like – let alone love! As Paul taught another local church, love is a fruit of God's Spirit. As we allow him to have greater control in our lives, he will do his work of fruit production (see Gal. 5:22–26).

Paul's strong feelings remain the same whether he is in prison (as now) or out and about on his missionary travels because he and the believers at Philippi are shareholders in God's grace (verse 7). They were joined to God and each other through the initiative of love demonstrated by Jesus' death on the Cross. Their bonding went beyond human friendship – it was the product of the Holy Spirit's work.

How do we view relationships within our own congregation – or with Christians from other churches? Are these positive experiences which lead us to thanksgiving and praise? Can we thank God every time we remember such people?

Questions

1. Think of some people who could be described as your partners in the gospel. How can you be practical in showing what partnership means?

2. Do you have friends you genuinely thank God for? Why not tell them or write a letter expressing your gratitude – it will help you and encourage them!

3. How can your local church develop stronger relationships?

Partners together

The concept of partnership comes through strongly in Paul's letter to the church at Philippi. In 1:5 he speaks of their 'partnership in the gospel' (literally fellowship or 'sharingship'). Paul viewed them not as clients or members of 'his' congregation – but as partners with him.

There are several examples where the idea of partnership is seen in the letter:

Partnership in the Gospel	1:5 Paul views them as his partners
Partnership in prayer	1:4 Paul prays for them 1:19 They pray for Paul
Partnership in the battle	1:27 They need to stand together 1:30 They are engaged in the same struggle as Paul
Partnership in servanthood	2:4 Servanthood is expressed through relationships.
Partnership in witness	2:14–16 They are called to let their lives witness together as bright lights in a dark world.
Partnership in sharing	4:14–19 The Philippians had consistently shown that partnership is a two-way process and must be demonstrated through practical care.

3

Philippians 1:9–11

Paul's prayer

Paul tells the Philippians what he has been praying for them.

Perhaps you have been through a difficult time when a friend has said: 'I have been praying for you' and you felt strengthened by their concern. The Christians in Philippi were facing problems and Paul feels it is important at the start of his letter to assure them they are on his prayer list.

There were tensions in the church which threatened their unity and they probably felt low in spirit that their founder and friend, Paul, was in prison facing the threat of the death penalty. Recognizing these twin pressures of disunity and discouragement, Paul writes this letter. He begins by assuring them of his prayer support and explaining what he is asking God to do for them.

His prayer request comes in four parts – all of them focussing on the *growth* of the Philippians. Paul is asking God that they might grow:

> In love (verse 9)
> In knowledge (verse 9)
> In discernment (verse 10)
> In holiness (verses 10–11)

Love   Paul's request is 'that your love may abound more and more' (verse 9)

He uses the word love (*agape*) in its broadest sense; love for God, love for fellow Christians and love for unbelievers. Love is the greatest of the Christian virtues – without it we are empty (see 1 Cor. 13:1–3, 13; 1 Thess. 3:12). The word translated *abound* suggests wealth and overflow and Paul uses the present tense indicating that we can never get enough of it. Growing in love must never stop for a believer.

Knowledge   Paul is praying that the Philippians will grow 'in knowledge and depth of insight ...' (verse 9).

As their love grows, he wants their knowledge of God, his character and ways, to increase. This is something Paul prays for other Christians as well (see Eph. 1:17; Col. 1:9–10). He obviously sees it as a key element of growing in faith. This is not simply an intellectual exercise of collecting facts about God, but an intimate knowledge of him. Rather like you would get to know a friend or a lover. Notice how Paul has linked together growing in love *and* growing in knowledge. The word translated by the phrase '*depth of insight*' (verse 9) means having the skill of knowing how to act in a particular situation, so this knowledge of God is to be shown by wise living.

Discernment   Paul prays 'that you may be able to discern what is best ...' (verse 10).

He is concerned that they learn to make right choices in their daily lives. Choosing right actions and avoiding wrong ones is a large part of discernment as well as being able to spot the true and the false. Like someone testing a counterfeit coin, he wants them to avoid being taken in by anything or anyone.

The Christians living in Philippi (just like Christians today) would constantly face difficult questions. Some would be to do with *belief*, some to do with *behaviour* and some to do with both! Paul is praying that their love and knowledge will increase to the extent that they will know how to choose 'What is best' in any given situation.

Holiness   Paul's longing for the Philippians is that they 'may be pure and blameless until the day of Christ' (verse 10).

He is looking ahead to the day when the Lord Jesus will return and is reminding his friends of their responsibility (and his) to keep morally clean. There is a positive and a negative side to this. Positively, being pure indicates aiming for the best. Negatively, being blameless means avoiding any charge of wrong behaviour. The way we behave as disciples of Jesus is very important. Holiness is not an optional extra but evidence that we are serious about following Christ. The return of Jesus is often used in the New Testament as a challenge to right living (see 1 Cor. 1:7–9; 2 Pet. 3:10–14). Paul describes holy living in terms of a harvest. This fruit comes 'through Jesus Christ–to the glory and praise of God' (verse 11). This is exactly the same truth that Jesus taught (see Jn. 15:5–8).

Paul's prayer agenda for the congregation at Philippi serves as a useful check list for ourselves and the local church to which we belong. Are we going for growth or content to stand still? Perhaps the need for more love, knowledge, discernment and holiness should figure in our prayers.

Questions

1. *How can we pray more intelligently for our local church? What are the major issues for prayer that you can recognize?*

2. *Spend some time reflecting on your own walk with God. What areas for growth would you add to love, knowledge, discernment and holiness?*

3. *'Live now in the light of then'. How should the fact that Jesus is coming back affect the way I live today?*

A profile of a local church

Philippi was the first church Paul planted in Europe. From Paul's letter we discover several striking parallels with local churches in today's world. Things may have changed a great deal in 1,900 years but people have not!

As we look over Paul's shoulder we get a picture of the problems and pressures faced by the Philippian congregation. In looking at their profile as a local church we perhaps discover how like them our church looks!

Here are some of the major local church issues Paul deals with:

Unity   There were tensions in the church because leading members had fallen out. Others were being affected and taking sides. The congregation was in danger of losing its way by fighting each other instead of the real enemy. The root of the issue was selfishness and a lack of the servant-like Spirit of Jesus (see 4:2–3; 1:27; 2:1–11).

Holiness   It was tough being a Christian in a society that had no time for Jesus. The pressure was always there to go along with the crowd. Some were finding it hard to live up to the standards expected of a Christian and wondered if it was worth going on (see 2:12–16; 4:8–9; 1:28–29).

Giving   They were a generous church who cared for others and showed it in practical ways. Their giving was a sacrifice, and some perhaps were worried about making ends meet. Then there was always the pressure to follow the world's standards and find your security in what you owned (see 4:10–20; 4:6–7; 3:20–21).

Leadership   Everyone accepted that good leadership was important. But other congregations had been disrupted by some very strange teaching from leaders who were only out to build their own power base. How could you spot the good from the bad (see 2:19–30; 3:1–3; 1:15–18)?

Faithfulness   When people first become Christians there is that first flush of enthusiasm. You can't get enough of meetings and Bible Study. But once a few years have passed things can get into a bit of a rut. There were things that had happened that had knocked people's faith. Something was missing, but no-one seemed to be quite certain what it was (see 1:21; 1:6; 1:9–11; 3:12–21).

Suffering   Why do bad things happen to good people? Is God really in control? If he is, then why do some situations turn out the way they do? There were times when these questions dominated the agenda, and perhaps made some begin to have doubts as to whether this Christian gospel was really true after all (see 1:12–26; 4:4; 4:13; 3:17; 4:19).

HOW TO LIVE AND HOW TO DIE
Philippans 1:12–26

4

Philippians 1:12–19

Paul's attitude to his circumstances

Paul begins his news report with a positive explanation of how God is bringing good things from a bad situation.

Paul was a man with a positive perspective on his circumstances. He knew the congregation at Philippi would be concerned to know how he was coping. The news that the apostle was in prison had, no doubt, made many of them feel despondent. Paul wastes no time in getting on with his personal news report.

He is quick to point out that what has happened to him has not held up the spread of the Christian message – on the contrary, the good news about Jesus ('gospel') is making great progress (verse 12).

He explains the reasons for his optimism which is based on some solid facts. First, some surprising people have had the opportunity to hear about the Lord Jesus Christ. Paul refers to the 'palace guard' (verse 13) who have come to learn that the reason for his imprisonment is his devotion to Christ. Paul lost no time in passing on his faith to those who guarded him and the result was that a group of unreached people were brought into contact with one of God's best spokesmen.

Second, he points out that other Christians have been stirred into action (verse 14). Paul was an effective Christian leader and his efficiency perhaps led others to stand back and let him get on with it as he seemed to do everything so well. But his enforced absence had spurred other believers to take up some of the responsibilities that Paul had been forced to lay down. They had discovered a new courage and boldness as a result.

A third reason for Paul's positive outlook is that Jesus Christ is being preached (verse 18). He has already mentioned believers that have been stirred into action in his absence. They have got involved with good motives ('goodwill': verse 15). Others are driven by less pleasant ambitions ('envy and rivalry': verse 15). Paul exposes the selfishness that lies at the heart of such unkind behaviour. We can only speculate at who Paul is referring to. Obviously there was a group of people who were in some way pleased that he was out of the way, leaving them a clear field. Perhaps some of these envious evangelists wanted to make a name for themselves and blacken Paul's reputation at the same time (verse 17).

The apostle's response to such behaviour is astonishing: 'But what does it matter?' (verse 18). He is not losing any sleep about it. From what we know of Paul he was never afraid to challenge things he believed to be wrong. He was even willing to risk friendships for a point of principle (see Acts 15:36ff; Gal. 2:11ff). He was never a man who avoided controversy in favour of a quiet life. Yet in this case it seems he is not wanting to take his opponents on. We see the reason in verse 18; what Paul cares about most of all is that the good news about Jesus is being announced everywhere. Some set about this all-important business with good motives, others with bad ones; but Paul is not distracted from the end result ... more people are hearing about Jesus Christ and that gives him the greatest joy.

It is important to understand that Paul is not simply 'looking on the bright side' by indulging in some positive thinking. His imprisonment must have filled him with anxiety at times, but his belief that God was working through his difficult circumstances helped him to recognize some positive gains his imprisonment had produced. Paul was a 'big-picture' Christian who knew when to stand back and see the hand of God drawing on a larger canvas. Paul is not preoccupied with himself; what stands out clearly from these verses is that the progress of the Christian message is his primary concern.

Paul is learning the truth of his own teaching; 'And we know that in all things God works for the good of those who love him who have been called according to his purpose' (Rom. 8:28). God is never taken by surprise when bad things happen to his children. He is able to work for our good in 'all things' that happen to those who have been drawn into his family. Paul was working this out in practice and drawing inner strength from the Spirit of Jesus and the encouragement of the prayers of God's people (verse 19). His hope is that he will eventually be released from prison – but in the meantime he is content to rest in the truth that God is bringing good things from a bad situation.

Questions

1. *What can we learn from Paul's personal example about facing difficult situations?*

2. *Is it ever right to confront people about wrong things in a local church – and are there times when we should say 'what does it matter?' How can we tell which response is appropriate?*

3. *Can you identify areas where the gospel is advancing today either in your own experience or across the wider world?*

Palace guard

Paul refers to the 'palace guard' (verse 13): the margin of the NIV supports an alternative translation could be 'the whole palace'. Paul uses the word *praetorium* which could be either applied to a building or a group of people, and this has prompted much discussion. Various ideas have been put forward including:

1 Caesar's Royal Palace
2 The barracks attached to the Palace itself
3 A large military camp or
4 A unit of soldiers known as the Praetorian Guard.

The last interpretation is the most widely accepted. The Praetorian Guard numbered around 9,000 seasoned soldiers who formed the Roman Emperor's personal bodyguard. In addition to guarding the Imperial Palace they were given other important duties.

Even if Paul is writing from the circumstances of house arrest rather than a prison cell he would probably have been guarded by squads from the Praetorian Guard – this may have involved being continually handcuffed to a soldier, (see Acts 28:20).

This round-the-clock guard duty as Paul waited for his court appearance would mean that a large group of soldiers would have met Paul and his frequent visitors and would have been able to listen in to his bold preaching (see Acts 28:30–31). This was a rare opportunity for such men to hear about Jesus Christ. They were a captive audience and this gives us an understanding of Paul's buoyant enthusiasm concerning the way God is using his time in prison.

The church at Philippi – how it all began

Dr Luke gives a dramatic account of Paul's first visit to Philippi (see Acts 16:11–40). This visit took place during his church-strengthening and church-planting tour which is often referred to as *Paul's Second Missionary Journey*. This took place around AD 49–52.

Having been directed to the province of Macedonia through a vision (Acts 16:9–10) Paul and his ministry team arrived at the influential city of Philippi.

Paul and his team began their evangelistic outreach on the banks of the Gangites River outside the city gates. A merchant-businesswoman named Lydia became a Christian and she offered Paul and his team hospitality in her home.

While they were staying in Philippi, Paul and Silas were caught up in an ugly mob attack sparked off by the exorcism of a young slave-girl. Her furious owners stirred up the crowd against the two foreigners – no doubt fuelled by a large measure of racial prejudice mixed with the pain of financial loss.

The result was that the city magistrates were called in. Ignoring the need for a fair trial to get to the root of the riot, they ordered that Paul and Silas should be publicly flogged and thrown into the jail at Philippi.

Despite a severe beating, Paul and Silas were praying and singing in the middle of the night when a violent earthquake hit the prison. Supernaturally the cell doors were opened and the prisoners' chains came loose. The jailer, fearing all his prisoners would escape, chose to commit suicide rather than face the consequences. Paul prevented him from doing this and as a result the jailer and his whole family became Christians.

The following day, the magistrates ordered their release. But Paul protests that his human rights as a Roman citizen have been violated. The magistrates were panic-stricken – they had not realized Paul and Silas were Roman citizens. The implications were very serious. Public beating for a Roman citizen was illegal, let alone a beating without a proper trial!

At Paul's insistence the magistrates themselves came to the prison to apologise and escort them out. This was more than Paul acting out of a sense of injured pride. It is probable he wanted to establish his innocence in order to 'buy time' for the new Christian congregation at Philippi and ensure some sort of official tolerance.

Paul's close attachment to the Philippian church is understandable given these circumstances. He carried on his body physical scars that reminded him of the cost attached to bringing the good news of Jesus to the city (see Gal. 6:17).

5

Philippians 1:20–26

Paul's attitude to life and death

Paul reveals his personal approach to living and dying and demonstrates his deep faith in Jesus.

The Apostle Paul was no stranger to tough situations (see 2 Cor. 11:23–29) and his present plight of facing possible execution was just another in a long catalogue of hazards. He shares with his friends in Philippi a personal glimpse into what made him tick. It is quite rare for Paul to indulge in such personal insights but he has a clear reason for doing so. This section is a personal testimony as Paul discloses his purpose for life, his philosophy of life and his predicament in life.

He is aware of the possibility that he could – in the face of martyrdom – let the Lord Jesus Christ down. But he is trusting God that when the time comes he will have the courage required (verse 20).

He speaks of his **purpose for life** that 'Christ will be exalted in my body whether by life or by death' (verse 20). He knows his trial before the Emperor could go either way – he may be facing immediate release or instant execution. But he has one clear goal in life and neither option can shake it; he wants the Lord Jesus Christ to be magnified through his whole personality.

Paul tells the Philippians his **philosophy of life** in a memorable phrase:

'For to me to live is Christ and to die is gain' (verse 21)

It is important to remember this is not empty rhetoric, uttered by someone living a life free from difficulties and making a high-sounding religious remark to impress his audience. Paul had lived the truth of what he is writing for many years. He had lost everything (status, friendships, reputation, freedom) for the sake of following Jesus (see 3:7) and now he was running the risk of losing his very life. But Paul believed what he taught others. Christ had given him new life (see 2 Cor. 5:17) and not even death itself could break this powerful new relationship (see Rom. 8:38–39). We sometimes hear someone say, 'he lives for his family/career/hobby', but when death strikes these things are beyond enjoyment. By contrast Paul can confidently assert that he is living for Jesus Christ and death cannot rob a believer of this best of all relationships.

Paul turns to his **predicament in life**. He is a man spoilt for choice, he does not know which is better, life or death! Paul is writing about a genuine dilemma he faced – something which caused him to ask deep questions as he felt pulled in opposite directions. 'I am torn between the two' (verse 23) describes his predicament. If God spares his life he will be able to carry on his busy ministry which he knows will continue to produce a spiritual harvest in peoples' lives (verse 22). But there is another heavy tug on his heart – he longs to be with the Lord Jesus whom he has followed for so many years. He sees this as 'better by far' (verse 23). He describes death in an interesting way by using the word translated 'depart' (verse 23) which conveys the idea of a group of soldiers breaking camp, or a ship loosing its moorings and raising the anchor in preparation to sail. In both cases the picture is one of moving on. Paul believed and taught (as did the other writers of the New Testament) that, for a Christian, the grave is not a cul-de-sac but a journey. Unselfishly, Paul recognizes that for the church in Philippi, and all the other congregations that benefited from his pastoral care, it is better that God allows him to continue his ministry on earth a little longer (verse 24). He seems to have a quiet belief that he will shortly be released from prison and able to make a return visit to Philippi in the near future. He believes this will be a time of great celebration and a means of encouraging the Christian believers in Philippi to go on in their faith (verse 26).

We are allowed a privileged glimpse behind the scenes in these verses to see beyond Paul the Leader into the heart of Paul the Christian. Perhaps that is a helpful reminder that our own leaders are flesh and blood people with their own joys and struggles. Do we always appreciate that as we pray for them and support their work?

Paul's personal testimony also challenges us about our response to problems. Paul had a firm grasp on the truths of the Christian faith. These were fixed points which helped him keep his bearings – even when the sea of life got choppy! He knew the answer to life's two great questions: 'Why am I here?'

'What happens when I die?'

For Paul, Jesus Christ, God's Son, provided the answer to both. Paul was a man who knew how to live and how to die and the single source of his confidence was *Jesus*. If you look back at the first twenty-six verses of this first chapter of Philippians you will notice how many times Paul refers to Jesus. This may help us understand what the Lord Jesus himself meant when he said, 'For out of the overflow of the heart the mouth speaks' (Mt. 12:34).

Questions

1. *If you were explaining your personal outlook on life and death to a non-Christian what would you say?*

2. *Do you appreciate the fact that the leaders in your church face personal struggles. How can you be more sensitive to their needs?*

3. *The great Scottish theologian, James Denney, once said 'we cannot at one and the same time show that we are clever and that Christ is wonderful'. What can we learn from Paul's example about making much of Jesus?*

Where was Paul when he wrote Philippians?

The location Paul was in when he wrote his letter to the Philippians has been the subject of much discussion between New Testament experts. The answer to the question is not as straightforward as it may at first seem.

The single certain *fact* is that Paul was in prison somewhere when the letter was written (see 1:13). That is where the detective work begins! Paul was a man with quite a police record having been in jail in the following places:

1 Philippi   (Acts 16)
2 Jerusalem   (Acts 21:27 – 23:31)
3 Caesarea   (Acts 23:31 – 26:32)
4 Rome   (Acts 28:30–31).

Some would also add:

5 Ephesus   (Acts 19:23ff – it is not recorded that Paul was impris-
              oned, but some experts think it likely).

Numbers 3 and 4 – Caesarea and Rome – would appear to have the
strongest evidence in support, but, as they say, the jury is still out on
this one!

The traditional view is that Paul is writing from Rome during the
period described by Luke in Acts 28:30–31, under circumstances of
house arrest. Paul's references to the 'palace guard' (verse 13) and 'Caesar's household' (4:22) would lend this view some weight.

STANDING FIRM
Philippians 1:27–30

6

Philippians 1:27a

Be consistent!

Paul urges the Philippian believers to live up to their high calling as citizens of the Kingdom of God.

The congregation at Philippi had sent Paul a love-gift via one of their leaders, a man named Epaphroditus. He had brought Paul up to date with the news of the church – and it was not all good news. Like any local church, they had their share of problems. Paul begins to address some of these issues in a sensitive way.

He expresses the hope that he will eventually be released and make a return visit to their city (verse 25) but he is not arrogant about his plans. The phrase 'Whatever happens' (verse 27) indicates Paul's flexibility in regard to God's power to overrule. The Bible warns that we should always make our plans with the spirit of reverent submission. How helpful it would be if some Christians erased from their vocabulary those four explosive words 'God has told me ...!' (see Jas. 4:13–17).

The apostle wants the Philippian church to live up to the standards expected of those who follow Jesus. He is reminding them to live consistently. The word translated *conduct* is used to describe behaviour expected of a citizen of a state. Philippi was a Roman colony and there was much pride in the honour of possessing Roman citizenship. This pride was reflected in civic life through language, dress and customs. Paul seems to be suggesting a spiritual parallel. The Philippian believers should have an even greater sense of pride that they are called to be citizens of Christ's Kingdom and their behaviour should reflect this honour.

We may ask what does it mean to 'live a life worthy of the gospel of Christ' (verse 27)? We find the answer in the pages of the New Testament where standards expected of disciples of Jesus are clearly set out. But in the context of the problems being faced by the Philippian church there are at least two areas where Paul's challenge needed to be taken up.

It needed to be applied in the area of **relationships**. Living a life worthy of the gospel involves accepting other people on the basis that God accepts us. Social status, ethnic background, age, sex – none of these things are a barrier to God's grace reaching us. They must not be barriers in our attitudes towards others.

The Philippian believers lived in a class-conscious society, but the gospel had come and broken the barriers down. Lydia (the first recorded convert in the city) was an Asiatic merchant-business woman from the upper echelons of Philippian society. The anonymous slave-girl whose deliverance sparked off the public riot was probably Greek and came from the bottom rung of the social ladder. The jailer would have been a Roman citizen and represented the middle-class (see Acts 16: 11–40). Jesus Christ had taken such diverse people and brought them into a new community. Paul wants his friends to live up to this privileged position (see Eph. 2:11–22).

This truth also needed to be applied in the area of **personal behaviour**. The Philippians lived in a society that operated on its own standards and they were far from being godly. They were called as Christians to live according to God's standards and demonstrate holiness to a watching world. This is a constant challenge leaders placed before the first Christians. When people have neglected such basic teaching they have paid the price in wrecked lives (see Col. 3:5–14; 1 Jn. 3:4–10; 1 Pet. 2:1–3).

Paul wants the Philippians to be consistent Christians. This challenge faces us today if we are to avoid the sterility of nominalism where we have all the jargon but little of the reality. To be called to be a citizen of the Kingdom of God is a high calling that demands high standards.

Questions

1. *How do we make plans? What does it mean practically to develop a spirit of reverent submission in our everyday decisions?*

2. *Can you identify the main areas in your life where you need to apply God's standards to your personal behaviour?*

3. *Can you identify barriers in your local Church that need to be broken down. Are there people who are being overlooked?*

7

Philippians 1:27b–28

Learning to co-operate

Christians need to stand together and support each other in the battle.

When a local church is under pressure it is easy to lose sight of the importance of standing together. Paul has picked up news of tensions that had arisen at Philippi concerning a dispute between two leading members. This is why, at this point in his letter, he stresses the importance of standing together.

Whether or not Paul is able to make a return visit to their city, he longs to hear that they 'stand firm in one spirit contending as one man for the faith of the gospel' (verse 27). Even if they face opposition, they should not be afraid. God will ultimately vindicate his people and deal with those who have persecuted them (verse 28). Who were these opponents? We may not know their exact identity or precisely how they made life difficult for the believers in Philippi, but we do know that behind the hands of such people lay Satan and his evil forces. He is always opposed to any church or individual determined to go God's way. His attacks always follow one of two main routes. Route 1 means internal attacks such as divisions, false teaching, bad leadership, immorality. Route 2 represents external attacks like ridicule, hostility and outright persecution.

The apostle gives a timely reminder that the way to withstand such enemy assaults is by presenting a united front. It could be that Paul is thinking of a similar picture to the one he uses when he writes his letter to the Christians in the city of Ephesus (see Eph. 6:10–18). There he draws parallels between a soldier's armour and the weapons God gives to his people in the spiritual battle in which we are engaged. It is possible that the Roman soldiers who were guarding Paul gave him insight as to how Christians could stand and fight together rather than turn and fight each other. The Roman Legions were renowned for their iron discipline. Often when under attack they would close ranks, raise their large shields together and advance behind an impenetrable wall. It took both skill and courage to stand together but they were able to take ground as they advanced as one man. This may not be the exact picture Paul has in mind. Others have suggested he may have been thinking of gladiators battling in the arena against a common enemy. In either case the principle remains the same – Christians need to stand together, not alone!

Paul deals with the specific divisions in the church at Philippi later in his letter (see 4:2ff) but for now he wants to get the principle across without referring to any specific personalities. They need to concentrate on the real enemy and learn to develop a genuine oneness in spirit.

This is an unashamed call for teamwork. One of Satan's unchanging tactics is 'divide and conquer' and churches in every generation that have successfully withstood his attacks are those who have proved the value of standing together in friendship, prayer and practical support. 'United we stand, divided we fall' is an important principle for all of us to apply!

Questions

1. Can you think of any specific instances of opposition to Christians at the moment both in your area and in other parts of the world?

2. Does 'oneness in spirit' mean that Christians have to agree on everything? How can we maintain our distinctives without losing our unity?

3. Can you pinpoint ways in which your own church has been under attack? What lessons have you learned for future battles?

8

Philippians 1:29–30

Handling conflict

Following Christ involves believing in him, and being prepared to suffer for him.

The apostle Paul has been encouraging his friends in the church at Philippi to live up to their high calling and stand together against the forces that oppose them. He concludes this appeal with a reminder of the twin marks of God's gracious call. All Christians have this double-barrelled call to 'believe on Him' (Jesus) and also 'to suffer for Him' (verse 29). Paul views this as a rich privilege. Viewing suffering for Christ as a special gift may appear a startling thought but it is totally in line with what Jesus said about discipleship and what new converts were taught in the early days of the growth of the church (see Lk. 9:23–24; Acts 14:22).

If suffering is to be expected at times for followers of Jesus, Paul wants his friends to know it is not pointless. Suffering is to be viewed as 'for Him' (verse 29). Whatever trials and difficulties may be faced they can be given as an offering to Christ and as a special act of dedication to him. (Have *you* ever viewed enduring well under pressure as worship?)

Notice there is no trace of 'us and them' in what Paul is writing. He shares in the same struggle. The word translated as *struggle* (from which we derive the English word agony) gives the idea of a fight or contest. This is a powerful picture that is used in other places in the New Testament (see Col. 2:1; 1 Thess. 2:2; 1 Tim. 6:12; 2 Tim. 4:7; Heb. 12:1). Paul reminds the Philippians that he and they are in this contest together – that is why he stresses the importance of standing firm. Suffering should produce solidarity not separatism.

The Philippian believers were well aware of Paul's struggles in the *past* – they had witnessed some of these for themselves. When the gospel first came to their city, Paul and his travelling companion had been attacked by a mob, publicly flogged and thrown into prison. This was hardly the ideal opportunity to invite others to follow your example in following Christ! But some had become Christians as faith was born against the backcloth of a mighty conflict.

Paul reminds them that the same struggles continue in the *present*. Life had not quietened down either for Paul or the Philippians. This letter was not written from the tranquil ease of a sun-drenched island retreat! Paul faces an uncertain future – but sees himself still competing in the contest he first entered when he met the risen Jesus Christ on the road to Damascus.

Paul is helping the Philippian Christians to see that they were not unique, and we need that reminder as well. For a follower of Jesus, conflict is par for the course. There is no need to look for it or feel deprived when it is absent. Instead let us remember the serious warning Jesus gave in the Parable of the Sower:

> 'The one who received the seed that fell on rocky places is the man who hears the word and at once receives it with joy. But since he has no root, he lasts only a short time. When trouble or persecution comes because of the word, he quickly falls away.' (Matt. 13:20–21).

Perhaps we need to be more honest in our evangelism and in our discipling of new Christians by teaching that opposition, conflict, suffering and sometimes full-blooded persecution are not unusual – but normal (see 2 Tim. 3:12).

Paul's timely reminder that it is a privilege to suffer for Christ must be read in the light of all that he is saying in this section in verses 27–30. In order to stand firm in the conflict that faces all who follow Jesus we need to exercise consistency and practise co-operation. These were important elements of teaching that the church at Philippi needed to relearn as they faced internal and external pressures.

Questions

1. How do you understand the twin privileges of believing in Christ and suffering for Christ?

2. Are we honest enough in our evangelism and discipling of new Christians? How could our presentation of the cost of following Jesus be conveyed with sensitivity?

3. Reflect on what Paul has been teaching in verses 27–30. There was a lack of understanding at Philippi in the areas of consistency, co-operation and conflict. How do you (and your church) rate compared to them?

LEARNING TO SERVE
Philippians 2:1–11

9

Philippians 2:1-2

Look at yourself

Paul challenges the Christians at Philippi to take an honest look at themselves.

The second chapter of Philippians is probably the best known part of the whole book, especially verses 1–11. Sometimes these verses are read out of context so it is important to understand where this section fits into the letter as a whole.

Paul is developing the theme which began in 1:27 where he tells the Philippian church to be consistent in living up to their high calling. This means being willing to support others in the conflict and difficulties Christian believers often face. An important component in this sort of lifestyle is a servant heart. In this section of the letter Paul shows the Philippians how to develop a serving spirit which involves the way we view ourselves (verses 1–2); others (verses 3–4) and the Lord Jesus Christ (verses 5–11).

Paul was a preacher who knew how to grab people's attention. He is making an impassioned plea for the Philippians to live out what they believe. In four staccato phrases he says, in effect, 'if this is what you believe, then this is how you should behave.'

1 'If you have any encouragement from being united with Christ' (verse 1). Paul poses the question, 'does being a Christian encourage and help you? Do you have a reason to get out of bed each morning? If so, then this is how you should behave ...'

2 'if any comfort from His love' (verse 1)
He asks: 'does the love of God embrace you in the darkest moments of life? If so, this is how you must live ...'
3 'if any fellowship with the Spirit' (verse 1)
Paul questions, 'do you believe the Holy Spirit has come to live within you and has brought you into God's family? If so, as followers of Jesus, you need to act like this ...'
4 'if any tenderness and compassion' (verse 1)
He puts the point: 'has the love of Christ melted your hard heart, making you more aware of other people and their needs? Then this is what God wants you to be ...'

Paul is expecting a resounding 'yes' to each of his questions because he knew firsthand that his Philippian friends had received the good news about Jesus and had personally experienced encouragement, love, fellowship with the Holy Spirit and compassion. He was confident that they would see the point he is making four times over.

Paul asks them to 'fill up' his joy ('make my joy complete': verse 2) by pursuing three objectives:

1 'by being like minded' (verse 2) – united in mind
2 'having the same love' (verse 2) – united in heart
3 'being one in spirit and purpose' (verse 2) – united in purpose.

Paul has many reasons to thank God for the church at Philippi as they have given him much joy (1:3,4). But his strong urging here suggests he was more than a little concerned that the church's future was under threat. He is encouraging them to be united in mind, heart and purpose.

Christians in a local church will not agree on every issue but they must agree on their overall aims (unity of mind) if they are to see God blessing their work. Unity of heart means loving and accepting each other, particularly when strong differences of opinion arise. Unity of purpose is essential if we are to keep on track when pressures from the inside and outside clamour for our attention.

Paul's lesson on servanthood begins with a call to a radical self-examination. Do we live out what we believe? Are we striving towards unity of mind, heart and purpose or are these ideals that we all too easily give up chasing? For the Philippians, and for us, learning to serve begins with an honest self-assessment.

Questions

1. Is self-examination always a good thing?
2. Are there areas where the unity of your local church is being tested? What part can you play to preserve that unity?
3. How can Christians express servanthood to those outside the church? Can you think of some practical examples in wider society of Christian servanthood in action?

10

Philippians 2:3–4

Look at others

Paul suggests two ways in which we should look at other people.

In order to develop a servant heart we need to have a proper view of other people. Paul is well aware that fallen human nature distorts the way we look at others. Some people feel less capable than others, believing that they could never match their standards. Others go through life in the belief that they are better than everyone else. Whether the problem is one of feeling inferior or superior, Paul's advice to the Philippians deserves careful attention. He proposes two ways in which the Christian believers at Philippi should view others in the church.

With humility

> 'Do nothing out of selfish ambition or vain conceit, but in humility consider others better than yourselves.' (verse 3)

Selfish ambition and vain conceit are two major driving forces in our lives. Paul has already mentioned some people who are dominated by them (see 1:17). Like untamed stallions they need to be broken in and controlled. Perhaps the Philippian Christians had become caught up in power politics where some were pushing their self-interest to the extreme. We are reminded that humility means considering others better (i.e. 'more important') than ourselves which is the perfect antidote to arrogance. In the Kingdom of God the way up is the way down. Jesus said: 'For everyone who exalts himself will be humbled, and he who humbles himself will be exalted.' (Luke. 18:14)

Even if we are not guilty of putting people down with our words, we can do it by our attitude. Paul tells the Philippians to lift people higher in their estimation and put themselves lower.

With unselfishness

Each of you should look not only to your own interests, but also to the interests of others (verse 4)

It is important to grasp what Paul is *not* saying. He is not telling the Philippians to neglect their jobs, families and personal welfare – that would be foolish in the extreme. He *is* encouraging them not to look after their own affairs alone, but to have an eye to how other people are getting on as well. He is wanting to see a sensitivity to other people's needs being developed and this means more than showing a passing interest. The implication of this whole section of the letter is that it costs to care. For the Philippians (and for us too) servanthood has a price-tag.

Our age has been described as the 'me-first generation', where pride and self-centredness are seen as virtues. Paul's words to the church at Philippi challenge such a view. Unless we treat other people with humility and unselfishness we can never fully discover what servanthood means. There were tensions in Philippi between people who were proud and selfish. Such tensions recur wherever people put themselves at the centre of their universe. How do *we* view others?

Questions

1. *Think for a moment beyond your own country, of the world-wide church ... how can we exercise humility and unselfishness towards them?*

2. *How practical is the instruction to look 'also to the interests of others?' Is there any sense of rivalry between the churches where you live? How can this be overcome?*

3. *Can you identify any examples of selfish ambition or vain conceit in the past week (for example, in your own life, family, job, or an example from the media etc.)?*

11

Philippians 2:5–11

Look at Jesus

Paul paints a picture of Jesus – the greatest servant who has ever lived.

Paul turns to the finest example of servanthood that has ever lived – the Lord Jesus Christ. He paints a vivid portrait of Jesus by quoting an early Christian hymn (verses 6–11: notice the way these verses are laid out in the N.I.V. translation as a quotation). This was more than likely a set of statements about Jesus that formed a creed or confession. The structure and style of the words suggest it was used in Christian worship as a written prayer or creed might be today.

Paul may or may not have been the author of it, but he quotes it as something his Philippian readers would have probably been familiar with. He is reminding them of the central truths of the Christian faith, and provides us with one of the finest passages in the New Testament about the Lord Jesus Christ. He introduces the quotation with a strong request:

'Your attitude should be the same as that of Christ Jesus' (verse 5)
(Literally translated: 'think the same way as Christ Jesus did')

Paul has challenged the Philippians' attitude towards themselves and towards others. This would probably have made them aware of their failures, so Paul points them to the best example to follow, that of the Lord Jesus. But he does so in such a way that they will not be crushed by their failures but challenged to do better by God's grace.

The hymn begins by describing the **position Jesus held**:

> Who, being in very nature God, did not consider equality with
> God something to be grasped (verse 6)

Paul asserts that Jesus was in his very nature, God. He was equal to
God but did not see that equality as something to cling on to, because it
was his by right. This was the startling claim of the first Christians, that
Jesus of Nazareth was God in the flesh. (The word *incarnation* is from
two Latin words which mean *in flesh*). He had existed with God from
eternity and his equality with the Father and the Holy Spirit was
understood and taught by other writers of the New Testament (see
Heb. 1:3–4; 2 Pet. 1:17–18; Rev. 1:9–18). The hymn Paul is quoting goes
on to describe the **position Jesus took** (verses 7–8).

Jesus 'made himself nothing' (verse 7) (literally 'he emptied himself').
He laid aside his heavenly glory (See Jn. 17:4); his riches (2 Cor. 8:9); his
independence (Jn. 5:30); and his favourable relationship to God's law (1
Pet. 2:24).

Jesus humbled himself 'taking the very nature of a servant' (verse 7)
(the word means 'slave'). He did not stop being God in order to be a servant but he demonstrated his very God-ness as a slave. He chose to
humble himself as a man even to the humiliating and painful death on a
cross. This was obedience, humility and unselfishness at its very limits.

For a Jew to die on a cross was a sign that a person was under God's
curse (Gal. 3:13; Dt. 21:23); to the educated Greeks it was ridiculous that
a so-called powerful God should die such a humiliating death (I Cor.
1:23) and in Roman society the word 'cross' was an obscenity you could
not mention in polite company. But Jesus humbled himself to take the
lowest place.

The hymn concludes with a great crescendo by describing the **position Jesus has** (verses 9–11). God exalted Jesus through the resurrection. The first Christians pointed to the historic fact of the empty tomb
as God's seal of approval on Jesus of Nazareth (see Acts 2:32–33; 4:10;
17:31).

He has been raised to 'the highest place' (verse 9) at the right hand of
God – a position of power and authority (Heb. 1:3) and given 'the name
that is above every name' (verse 9).

In New Testament times a name not only distinguished someone
from another person, it revealed something of their nature. In raising
Jesus to his right hand God conferred on him his own name of LORD
(*Yahweh* or Jehovah), the personal name God revealed himself through
in the Old Testament.

Looking ahead to the end of history as we know it, the hymn declares that one day every knee will bow 'at the name of Jesus' (verse 10) and 'every tongue confess that Jesus Christ is Lord to the glory of God the Father' (verse 11).

Even those who deny him and use the name of Jesus Christ as an expletive will confess his undisputed claim to be Lord of the universe. This honour is doubly his. It belonged to Jesus before the world began, it has now been given to him as a gift of God because of his exaltation (see Mt. 28:18; Eph. 1:20–21).

We need to pause for breath and to wonder at who Jesus is and all that he has accomplished for us through his death on the cross. Truly, he deserves our worship. But we must ask a question: why does Paul choose this part of this letter to the Philippian church to quote this powerful hymn?

He has been painting a picture of the greatest servant that ever lived. Jesus laid aside his own interests – so should we. He served others by putting them first – we should follow his example.

The Philippian church needed to deal with the pride and selfishness that existed among them. Paul's picture of Jesus encouraged them to cultivate the same attitude that he had shown by coming to this earth as a baby (verse 5).

Servanthood begins with a proper evaluation of ourselves, a correct attitude towards others and a genuine commitment to follow the example of Jesus in our daily actions.

Perhaps we, like the Philippians, feel overwhelmed at such a tall order as this! Who could ever expect to live a life like Jesus? But notice how Paul began this section by reminding his friends of the truth that they were united with Christ through the fellowship of the Spirit (verse 1). Paul is urging them to be *like* Jesus because they are *part of* Jesus. It is his power that enables them to follow his example. As one writer has put it, servanthood 'should be the imitation of a child exhibiting family traits!'

If we wish to become servant people in the church and in the world, we would do well to study Paul's wise words and allow the hymn about Jesus to inspire us to change.

Questions

1. *Spend a few minutes reading and reflecting on the 'hymn' in verses 5–11. Then use the words as a basis for your own worship and appreciation of the Lord Jesus Christ.*

2. *Consider how your local church can fulfil the words of 1 John 2:6, 'Whoever claims to live in him must walk as Jesus did'.*

3. *The theme of 2:1–11 is servanthood. How can you 'improve your serve' in your local church?*

An early Christian hymn

It is widely agreed by New Testament experts that Philippians 2:6–11 is an early Christian hymn. It has an easy rhythm about it and appears to be laid out in six stanzas of three lines each.

The theme of the hymn is the Lord Jesus. It explains who he is, why he came, what he did and where he is now. It may have been used to teach new believers the foundational facts of the Christian faith – possibly being used at the Lord's Supper (Communion) or for baptisms. Whether Paul wrote it or is borrowing it from elsewhere is not that important.

This hymn gives us one of the finest passages in the New Testament about the Lord Jesus Christ. It is rich in spiritual truth. Yet the context is a very practical one where Paul is urging Christians to stop following selfish ambition and vain conceit and, instead, to follow the servant-like example of Jesus. This reminds us that theology and Christian living belong together and must not be pushed apart.

There are other examples in the New Testament of hymns or creeds (a concise statement of Christian 'basics' used to teach new believers) being used or quoted. Here are some examples; Ephesians 4:4–6; 1 Timothy 1:17; 3:16; 6:15; 2 Timothy 2:11–13.

Who is Jesus?

Philippians 2:5–11 is one of the key passages in the New Testament that deals with who Jesus is. (The branch of Theology that deals with who Jesus is and what he achieved through his death and resurrection is known as *Christology*.)

The verses trace the life of Jesus from eternity past (verse 6), through his birth (verse 7), death (verse 8), resurrection and ascension (verse 9) to eternity future (verse 10–11).

What is remarkable is that Paul makes these bold assertions within thirty years of Jesus' execution in Jerusalem. Paul was no starry-eyed follower of Jesus who could not cope with the finality of his Master's death and so allowed the rumour to spread that he had miraculously risen from the dead. Paul (or Saul as he was known then) was a serious-minded Jew with no time for Jesus of Nazareth. He was of the opinion that the claim made by the followers of Jesus that he was the divine Son of God who had risen from the dead was nothing less than blasphemy. That a man with Paul's background had come to believe these truths about Jesus is truly astonishing!

It is also important to notice that Paul is quoting these words to his friends at Philippi on the assumption that they accepted them as true statements. He is not setting out to make a case for the Divinity of Jesus. He is talking about Christians following Jesus' example by living humble lives – but in doing this he reminds his readers of some foundational truths about who Jesus is.

What Paul is saying here

- Jesus of Nazareth was in very nature God and equal with God (verse 6)
- Jesus emptied himself by becoming a man and taking the very nature of a servant (verse 7) (He didn't stop being God; his emptying came in taking to himself human nature)
- His humble obedience led him to lay down his life on the cross (verse 8)
- God raised Jesus up from death and exalted him to the highest place – the right hand of God (verse 9)
- God has given him the name above every name – the LORD (*Yahweh* or Jehovah) (verse 9)
- At the end of this present age all will acknowledge his ultimate Kingship to the glory of God the Father (verses 10–11)

Some other important passages in the New Testament

There are several New Testament passages that make a clear assertion that Jesus is Divine: Romans 9:5; Hebrews 1:8; John 1:1–12; John 1:18; Titus 2:13; John 20:28; 2 Peter 1:1; Acts 20:28.

There are other passages that imply the same truth: Matthew 1:23; John 17:3; Colossians 2:2; 2 Thessalonians 1:12; 1 Timothy 1:17; James 1:1; 1 John 5:20.

Certainly the first disciples were convinced about Jesus' claim to be the Son of God – and wanted others to know him too (see Jn. 20:30–31; 2 Pet. 1:16–18).

For those who assert that Jesus never claimed to be God and that the disciples either mistook or misrepresented his words, there remains the charge laid against him by the Jewish authorities that ultimately led to his execution by the Roman governor. The charge was blasphemy, that he claimed to be the Son of God (see Mt. 26:60–68; Lk. 22:66–71).

If there was any chance that Jesus had been misquoted he would have cleared up the misunderstanding – particularly when faced with the threat of crucifixion.

HOW TO BE HOLY
Philippians 2:12–18

12

Philippians 2:12–13

Three vital ingredients

Paul teaches about the aim, attitude and assistance which make holy living possible.

Paul addresses the Christians at Philippi in the warmest terms; 'my dear friends' (verse 12 literally – 'my beloved'). He does so for a good reason, not merely to butter them up. He has been saying some difficult and challenging things and wants the congregation to know that this comes from a heart of love.

Love does not mean ignoring faults. Real love must be tough enough to point them out and tender enough to face the consequences (see Pr. 27:5–6).

In the past, when Paul has been in Philippi, they have responded to his teaching positively. He is encouraging them to an even quicker response of obedience now he is absent. He pleads with them to listen hard to all he has been saying about unity, humility, unselfishness and servanthood. To sum all these qualities up in a word, we would describe the end-product as *holiness*. This word is used throughout the Bible – but what does it mean? Holiness means becoming more like Jesus Christ in our attitudes, actions and behaviour. It must be the goal of every Christian disciple (see 1 Jn. 2:6). How can we achieve what seems to be way beyond our grasp – who could ever live as perfect a life as Jesus did?

Paul lifts the lid on this important subject in these two verses and gives us three vital ingredients to help us to strive to attain what appears at first to be unattainable.

The first ingredient is **the aim we are to take.**

'... continue to work out your salvation...' (verse 12)

It is important for us to understand that Paul is not suggesting that the salvation Jesus made possible through his death and resurrection is in some way incomplete. He is simply telling the Philippians to work out the implications of this wonderful gift in their daily lives. Salvation (which means to be 'made whole' through Christ) has three tenses:

Past 'I have been saved' (see Gal. 2:20)

Present 'I am being saved' (verse 12)

Future 'I will be saved' (see Phil. 3:21)

Paul is encouraging the Philippians to work on the present tense aspect of salvation. They must be clear in their aim that this salvation is to be worked out and applied each day; they are not to stand still but to grow in their faith.

A second ingredient is **the attitude we should adopt.**

'... with fear and trembling' (verse 12)

Paul uses two surprising words, 'fear and trembling', which suggest punishment rather than blessing. The two Greek words he uses give us words in the English language such as phobia and trauma which make holiness sound a very unattractive goal! But Paul is reminding the Philippians of a truth that runs through the Bible – holy living is a serious business. We are not to treat it casually or to make sin a laughing matter. God deserves and demands our respect (see Pr. 1:7; Ps. 2:11). Changing our behaviour to conform with God's pattern demands our full attention. Our relationship with God is the most important issue in the whole of life. Paul is writing about a healthy, motivating fear, not a destructive one. We instil in young children healthy fears of busy roads, playing with matches and talking to strangers. We perhaps know the motivating fear of a looming exam or a deadline for a piece of work. Such fears keep us safe and bring out the best in us. It is in this vein that Paul is telling the Philippians to adopt an attitude of serious intent so far as holy living is concerned.

The third and final ingredient Paul mentions is **the assistance that is available**.

'... for it is God who works in you to will and to act according to His good purpose' (verse 13)

He reminds the Philippians that they are not alone – God has promised them his help. He is working in their lives (see 1:6), giving them the desire to be different and helping that change take place. We are touching on a subject that has occupied Christians through the ages. How can we achieve a holy life? Is it all up to me with self-effort and discipline? Is it all up to God as I release my grasp on going it alone? Is there a 'special blessing' which produces the desired result and if so, how can I get the tape/read the book/attend the conference/hear the speaker/have someone pray over me (delete as appropriate!).

Look carefully at what Paul is saying in these verses. There are two sides to the coin of holiness. Out of the three ingredients we are expected to play our part (in aim and attitude) and God promises to play his (in assistance). Paul is encouraging his Philippian friends to press on in their faith, to pursue holiness with a relentless hunger to become more Christ-like and to recognize behind it all, God is willing and acting to achieve his 'good purpose' which is to produce people '... conformed to the likeness of his Son ...' (Rom. 8:29).

Questions

1. Read John 15:1–17. How do the words of Jesus shed more light on what Paul has been saying to the Philippians?

2. Are there specific areas in your life where you struggle to be holy? Have you brought these to God?

3. Do 'fear and trembling' have any part to play in worship, prayer or preaching?

4. Why does Paul stress the importance of the Philippians being obedient to his teaching in his absence (see 2:12)?

13

Philippians 2:14–18

Two pictures

Paul uses the pictures of stars in a dark sky and sacrifices on an altar to teach the importance and impact of holy living.

Most of us understand pictures more easily than concepts. Paul draws two vivid pictures to illustrate both the importance and the impact of holy living. The first picture is of *stars in a dark sky* (verses 14–16a.)

He instructs the Philippians to 'do everything without complaining or arguing' (verse 14) as they live in a 'crooked and depraved generation' (verse 15). This is a direct reference to the nation of Israel in the Old Testament who repeatedly complained about having left Egypt (see Dt. 32:5, 20). There could be a suggestion here that negativism had seized some of the church members in Philippi and they were criticizing their leaders as the children of Israel had done to Moses. Paul's call to holy living is so that they 'may become blameless and pure, children of God without fault ...' (verse 15). Paul's word-picture is of a dark sky dotted with thousands of pinpricks of light coming from the stars. In the same way that stars stand out against the dark sky so the Philippians were called to live holy lives in a corrupt society. In case we find Paul's description of his society as being over-critical, read again Jesus' analysis of his generation (see Mt. 12:39; 17:17). This is how God views any society that rejects him. Not that such an evaluation should make us smug or condemning. Paul reminds the Philippians that they 'hold out the word of life' (verse 16a). The Philippians may live in a morally dark world, but they are called to live differently (as 'animated question marks', as one writer has described our Christian duty to society), and by words and actions to show there is a better way to live.

The second picture is more difficult for us to understand – although the Philippians would have easily picked up Paul's meaning. He employs the picture of *sacrifices on an altar* (verses 16b–18). Paul is looking ahead to the time when Jesus will return – 'the day of Christ' (verse 16b) – when he hopes he will be able to feel proud about their spiritual progress. He wants to know that the time and hard work he has committed to their discipleship has paid off. Like an athlete in a race or a workman tackling a project, Paul needs to know that his energy has been well spent and that he did not 'run or labour for nothing ...' (verse 16b).

He speaks of himself being 'poured out like a drink offering on the sacrifice of service coming from your faith (verse 17), which the Philippians would have understood.

He uses a word which means 'to offer a drink offering'. It is only used twice in the New Testament, here and in 2 Timothy 4:6. When visiting a temple or shrine of a god, a worshipper would often pour wine or olive oil on the ground as an offering. When an animal was brought to the Temple at Jerusalem to be sacrificed, a drink-offering would often be poured over it. It was added last of all as a finishing touch. Paul's picture suggests that the Philippians' devotion to Jesus is both a sacrifice and a service. He sees his own life – the energy and devotion he has committed to sharing the Christian message – as a drink offering poured out on the offering that the Philippians represented. He sees his life in the context of their progress as Christian disciples. He considers his efforts on their behalf as a last word or finishing touch. There is no self-pity or false humility here. Far from it, Paul tells them how much he rejoices with them and trusts that they share that joy too (verses 17,18).

These two pictures help us understand why we should be motivated to be holy people. As stars set against a dark sky, we are called to witness to a lost world. As sacrifices on an altar we are called to give ourselves in service to the Lord Jesus. Through the centuries the pursuit of holiness has led some into blind alleys. Some have fallen into *legalism*, seeing holiness as a long list of rules and regulations to be strictly adhered to. Others have embraced *nominalism*, where private behaviour is kept separate from what is professed publicly. Some people have turned to *asceticism*, believing that depriving the body of comfort, food or sleep can subdue its desires.

But in the New Testament, holiness is seen as a reflex response to the kindness and mercy of God. Grace makes you grateful.

Holiness is motivated by love. It is a life lived in grateful response to God for his gift of Jesus. Holiness is a good thing. It makes me a better person, a better parent and partner, a better employer, employee, neighbour, friend and citizen. Holiness is good for you, good for society and – most important of all – it brings pleasure and glory to God.

Questions

1. What pictures can you draw from today's world to convey what holiness is and why it is so important?

2. Paul seems to suggest that the Philippian congregation were guilty of 'complaining and arguing'. Would he make the same comments about your church?

3. In what ways should the church 'hold out the word of life' in society?

4. Are there Christians who 'pour themselves out' on your behalf? Thank God for them and look for people you can invest time in.

GODLY LEADERSHIP
Philippians 2:19–30

14

Philippians 2:19–24

Timothy

Paul passes on some personal news about Timothy, and shows how his godly character is seen in the quality of his relationships.

At this point in the letter, Paul appears to suddenly change the subject and pass on some information concerning the travel plans of two people who were with him, Timothy and Epaphroditus. It is possible that Paul is not being side-tracked but is quite deliberately using these two men as living examples of what he has been
teaching. The qualities of holiness spelt out in the earlier part of Chapter 2, are demonstrated by Timothy and Epaphroditus.

He begins with Timothy, who is hoping to come to Philippi shortly as Paul's special envoy (verse 19). Paul is looking forward to receiving a first-hand report of the church which will encourage him while he awaits trial. Paul's plans are tentative in spite of his authority and years of experience, and he makes his plans carefully expressing his intentions by saying 'I hope in the Lord Jesus ...' (verse 19). (There may have been an important reason why Timothy could not leave Paul at this particular point.) He then goes on to give a character reference for Timothy which in one sense is unnecessary as the Philippians knew him well! But the way Paul writes suggests that he is using the opportunity to underline some of the truths he has mentioned earlier in his letter. Paul talks first about his **relationship to the church**: 'I have no-one else like him who takes a genuine interest in your welfare' (verse 20).

Paul uses a rare poetic word that appears nowhere else in the New Testament meaning 'of like mind, a kindred spirit.' He and Paul shared a very close relationship but Paul's commendation is not based on personal favouritism. Timothy is a man who displays a genuine interest in other people's well-being. He can be trusted with responsibility because he is not dominated by selfishness. He epitomizes what Paul has urged the Philippians to become in 2:4! Timothy is a flesh-and-blood example of looking after others' interests and not just your own. Paul may have been paving the way for Timothy to do some sorting out in the church at Philippi. If the divisions had not been dealt with by the time he arrived, Timothy may well need to tackle some individuals about their attitude. Paul underlines that Timothy's heart desire is to consider the welfare of the church.

Paul describes Timothy's **relationship with the Lord Jesus Christ**: 'For everyone looks out for his own interests not those of Jesus Christ'. (verse 21)

Some have suggested Paul may have been having a sideswipe at others who were with him in Rome that were not up to the task of visiting Philippi as Timothy was being asked to do, but that misses the point. Timothy is an outstanding Christian in Paul's estimation, a person who puts Jesus Christ first in all that he does. Timothy's loyalty and commitment were beyond question. The words of Jesus in the Sermon on the Mount would apply to him (see Mt. 6:33).

A third aspect of Timothy's character that is highlighted concerns **his relationship with Paul**: 'But you know that Timothy has proved himself, because as a son with his father he has served with me in the work of the gospel' (verse 22).

Paul had a unique relationship with Timothy (see *What do we know about Timothy?*) and some have suggested that this filled a gap in Timothy's own life owing to a weak relationship with his natural father. Paul refers to him here, and in other places as his 'son' which conveys how deep their friendship had gone (see 1 Tim. 1:2; 2 Tim. 1:2, 1 Cor. 4:17). There is no suggestion that this was a claustrophobic friendship – on the contrary. Timothy matured as a result of Paul's fatherly interest.

Paul reminds the Philippians that Timothy has 'proved himself' (verse 22) like a metal that has been tested and found to be pure. Timothy's track record was known to the Philippians. He had been with Paul when the church began (see Acts 16:1ff) and probably visited them on other occasions. He was a man with an established track record who had proved himself to be trustworthy. Paul commends his servant heart as he has worked alongside the apostle. Timothy (by now in his thirties probably) was a man who had served a good apprenticeship. This is a good reminder that character and gifting need to be tested and proved over a period of time.

Paul is hopeful that he will be able to send Timothy to Philippi, but not just at the present time as something appeared to be moving in relation to Paul's impending court appearance (verse 23). In any event, Paul remains quietly confident in God, hoping he will be released and able to visit Philippi personally (verse 24).

Questions

1. *How important is it that people 'prove' themselves before being entrusted with responsibility? How can a local church apply this in a way that doesn't discourage those who are keen to serve God?*

2. *Timothy's character could be seen in the quality of his relationships. What condition are your relationships in at present?*

3. *Paul invested years in discipling Timothy and the end product was a mature Christian leader. Is there someone God is asking you to pass on your experience to in preparation for bigger things to come?*

4. *Paul hoped to send Timothy to the Philippians as a personal bridge (2:19). Are such personal bridges needed between churches in today's world?*

What do we know about Timothy?

- He owed much to the women in his life; his mother (Eunice) and his grandmother (Lois) (Acts 16:1; 2 Tim. 1:5).
- His father was a Greek and not a believer.
- His mother was a Jewess who came to believe that Jesus was the Messiah.
- Paul meets him in Lystra. He had an excellent reputation among local Christians so Paul invited him to join his travelling ministry team – but only after Timothy had been circumcised (Acts 16:1–5).
- He travelled extensively with Paul as a travelling companion and developed as a Christian leader in his own right. They had a close 'father and son' friendship (Phil. 2:22).

- His name is mentioned in many New Testament letters (Phil. 1:1; Heb. 13:23; Rom. 16:21; 1 Cor. 4:17; 2 Cor. 1:1; Col. 1:1; 1 Thess. 1:1; 2 Thess. 1:1).
- He probably wrote as Paul dictated his letters. It is also possible that he and Paul had often discussed together what should be written so that it was a joint message.
- He would probably have visited Philippi on several occasions at the time the letter was written. He was with Paul when the church began (Acts 16:11ff).
- His strengths appear to be that he was warm, sensitive and dependable. His weaknesses are suggested as timidity and fear (2 Tim. 1:6ff).
- He has two letters in the New Testament that bear his name. These are two personal letters written to him by Paul giving excellent advice on being an effective Christian leader. Together with Titus they form what are know as the Pastoral Letters, because of the teaching given about being a good pastor or leader of God's people.

15

Philippians 2:25–30

Epaphroditus

Paul commends Epaphroditus – one of the Philippian leaders and a man who risked his life for Christ.

Having shared his plans for Timothy to visit Philippi, Paul introduces a second name, that of Epaphroditus. Even if Timothy cannot travel to Philippi just yet, a man called Epaphroditus is to take the letter Paul is writing. He needed no introduction to the Philippian congregation as he was one of their own leaders. The only references to him in the New Testament are found in this letter (see also 4:18), but we can piece together a sketch outline of what appears to have happened.

Epaphroditus was sent by the church as a courier carrying the money they had collected for Paul as a love-offering (verse 27; 4:18). The intention was probably that he would spend some time with Paul while he was in custody. Either on the journey or when he arrived in Rome, Epaphroditus fell seriously ill. The situation was so grave that he nearly died (verse 27). The Philippians had heard of his illness (verse 26) and so Paul is sending him back earlier than originally planned. His warm commendation of Epaphroditus could possibly be to deflect any criticism among the Christians at Philippi that he had not fulfilled his mission. (How quick we sometimes are to make rash judgments about people without knowing all the facts.)

The name Epaphroditus means 'lovely, charming and amiable' – it is derived from the name of the goddess Aphrodite and it is possible that his family had belonged to a group of people who worshipped her.

As a convert to Christianity Epaphroditus appears to have lived up to his name! Paul pays him a glowing tribute. He writes about his **character**, and uses five different descriptions of him all contained in verse 25:

'**My brother**'   which suggests a close relationship with Paul.

'**My fellow-worker**'   he was not a man to sit around doing nothing.

'**My fellow-soldier**'   Paul uses a military description for a 'comrade-in-arms', someone who has stood at your shoulder in the trenches.

'**Your messenger**'   Paul actually uses the word 'apostle', signifying Epaphroditus was acting as an ambassador on behalf of the Philippians.

'**Whom you sent to take care of my needs**'   Paul describes him as a 'minister' sent to give him practical help.

This assortment of job titles tell us that Epaphroditus was quite a man. He was loveable, diligent, courageous, trustworthy and possessed a servant heart. Paul provides more than a testimonial here – it is another living example of what holiness *is*.

Paul also writes of Epaphroditus' **compassion**: 'For he longs for all of you and is distressed because you heard he was ill' (verse 26).

Like Timothy, Epaphroditus had a heart for people. He missed his friends at Philippi and was concerned that they had been worried about him. But there may well be more to it. Paul uses a word translated *distressed* which means to be in great anxiety. The only other time it is used in the New Testament is in reference to Jesus in the Garden of Gethsemane (see Mt. 26:27; Mk. 14:33). It describes mental and spiritual anguish that often follows a great shock. Epaphroditus had brushed closely with death and was not fully over the trauma, so his desire to see his fellow Christians (and family?) in Philippi is understandable. We get something of the measure of the man when Paul suggests Ephaphroditus is distressed at their distress over him!

Paul is grateful that God spared Epaphroditus and is keen that he makes the homeward journey (verses 27, 28). It is a reminder that Christian service can be costly and dangerous and should never be seen as light entertainment. Epaphroditus had 'risked his life' (verse 30) in acting as the emissary of the Philippian church. No wonder Paul tells them to welcome him home and honour him (verse 29), although Epaphroditus may well have blushed with embarrassment as this part of the letter was read to the whole congregation in his presence!

Paul places Timothy and Epaphroditus side by side as examples of godly leaders. Undoubtedly they both had their weaknesses and failures, but they provided a model of the type of practical holiness Paul has been urging the Philippians to adopt.

Questions

1. *If someone was asked to write a character reference for you, what do you think it would say? Can you identify your personal strengths and weaknesses?*

2. *The Philippians were told to honour people like Epaphroditus. As you look around your local church are there individuals who deserve to be honoured? How can you go about it?*

3. *Some Christians risk their lives today for the sake of Christ (i.e. in countries where it is illegal to witness or even practise your faith). But for those who live in countries where there is no direct persecution, what does it mean to put our lives on the line for Jesus?*

4. *One of the greatest needs in the world church today is for leaders of quality. How can they be discovered and trained? Spend some time praying for those who give their time to this important task.*

Risk-takers

Epaphroditus, we are told, risked his life in order to minister to Paul. The word that is used has an interesting history; it is a verb which conveys the idea of exposing oneself to danger.

Some have suggested it has links with gambling where someone risks everything on the turn of the dice. In the Early Church there was a group of people called the 'gamblers' (a named based on the word Paul uses here). They visited the sick – particularly those with infectious diseases – and those in prison. In the city of Carthage in AD 252 a terrible plague raged, and many people died. Bodies were thrown into the streets as panic set in. A Christian leader named Cyprian organized his congregation to bury the dead and tend those who were dying of the plague. They put their own lives at risk as godly gamblers.

WHAT ARE YOU TRUSTING IN?
Philippians 3:1–11

16

Philippians 3:1–3

A warning

Paul gives a warning against a group of people who seek to rob Christians of their freedom in Christ.

This next section of the letter runs from 3:1–11 and contains a spirited defence of the Christian Gospel in which Paul shares something of his personal story of the radical changes that have taken place in his life since meeting Jesus Christ on the road to Damascus.

Paul appears to be drawing his letter to a close and is making a final appeal for the Philippians to 'rejoice in the Lord' (verse 1). He does not apologize for repeating himself, far from it, and he points out the safety of hearing important truths stated over and over again. But as he is about to sign off, he suddenly launches into a long digression (which probably runs to 4:4). This is not an unnecessary diversion – in fact it provides us with a key section of the whole letter packed with good things. As more than one writer has commented, if Paul had intended to finish the letter at this point, we can be grateful to the Holy Spirit for prompting him to keep going!

Paul gives a sudden warning: 'Watch out for those dogs, those men who do evil, those mutilators of the flesh' (verse 2). He writes the warning 'Look out!' no less than three times in this single verse. Who or what is Paul urging the Philippians to guard against?

He is probably referring to a group of people known as Judaizers (sometimes referred to as 'the circumcision party'). They created havoc in the early years of the growth of Christianity and many local congregations were left confused and divided by their teaching. They taught that faith in Jesus alone was not sufficient to save a person. They insisted that circumcision for men and observing other Jewish food laws and customs were required to make an individual acceptable to God. Paul does not hold back in his condemnation of them. He calls them 'dogs' which was the insulting title Jesus gave to Gentiles and Paul, with a twist of humour, turns it on them. He refers to them as 'evil workmen', intent on destroying God's work and, as a parting shot he does not even use the proper word for circumcision (an ironic reference to their insistence that men should be circumcised to become 'true' Christians), but instead calls them 'mutilators'.

Why such strong language from someone who preached about the love and mercy of God? It is because Paul saw the immense damage the Judaizers were causing. He regarded them as enemy agents whose evil task was to seek to add to the gospel and bring people under bondage of rules and regulations. They asserted that Jesus was not enough – that made them 'enemies of the cross' (verse 18) in Paul's estimation, and he was determined to oppose them at every turn.

Paul argues that those who belong to the true circumcision can be recognized by three characteristics. The Judaizers boasted about circumcision so much that it almost became a badge to them. Paul asserts that the circumcision God seeks is of the heart, not the body (see Rom. 2:28–29) and that is summed up in three ways.

'We who worship by the Spirit of God' (verse 3)

A true Christian is someone in whom the Spirit of God dwells. True worship is not an empty ritual based on observing man-made traditions but is done 'in spirit and in truth' (see Jn. 4:23–24).

'... who glory in Christ Jesus' (verse 3)

Paul pretends that the Judaizers are making less of Jesus, his death and resurrection. He believes that those who are spiritually circumcised (having 'cut off' and 'put away' their old life) are those who put all their trust in Christ.

'... and who put no confidence in the flesh ...' (verse 3)

At heart the Judaizers were trusting in themselves to obtain salvation. Their confidence was in their own actions. Paul asserts that true Christians rejected any reliance on their own efforts to save them.

We may not face the Judaizers today, but there are many who push a 'Jesus plus' message. Any group that claims the death and resurrection of Jesus is not sufficient to bring salvation is following the same destructive path the Judaizers took back in the first century AD. Paul's strong, uncompromising warning should help us to understand how any attempt to add to or take away from the authentic Christian gospel must be resisted at all costs.

Questions

1. Can you pinpoint any groups in the world today who present a 'Jesus plus' message? How should we respond to: a) the teaching; b) the people who are caught up in it?

2. Do you think there is a place for strong words and serious warnings today? Can you identify particular areas where such an approach is needed?

3. How can a local church stay on track and avoid the danger of buying a watered-down version of the Christian Gospel?

Judaizers – Who were they?

Judaizers were Jewish Christians who believed that a number of the ceremonial laws of the Old Testament were binding on the New Testament Church. In particular they insisted that Gentile men who wished to become Christians, had to submit to the Jewish rite of circumcision. (This is a relatively minor, but painful, piece of surgery where a small amount of skin is cut away from the tip of a man's penis.)

They may well have started with good intentions – seeking to win strict Jews to faith in Jesus as Messiah. Such people would be horrified to share fellowship with a Gentile, but if that person had converted to the Jewish faith and was 'wearing the badge of circumcision' a strict Jew would be more likely to accept them. The issue became so divisive that a special conference of the Church was called in Jerusalem in around AD 50. You can read Luke's report in Acts 15:1–35. The theological issue hinged on the Judaizers' insistence that a man could not be saved unless he was circumcised. The historic decision of the Jerusalem Council was to reject this view.

Paul became the leading opponent of the Judaizers and was the subject of their attacks. His letter to the Galatians was written against the background of their attempt to destabilise a group of Christian churches with their false gospel. Paul's strong language (see Gal. 5:12 and Phil. 3:2) must be understood against the background of his belief that Judaizers were saying that the death and resurrection of Jesus were not sufficient for salvation. Paul insisted that the authentic Christian 'Good News' stated that a person was justified (made right) by faith in Jesus Christ alone.

17

Philippians 3:4–6

The way I used to be

Paul shares his testimony and reveals the things he once trusted in to make him right with God.

Paul has told his Philippian friends that one of the distinguishing marks of a real Christian is a person's refusal to rely on their own ability to save themselves ('who put no confidence in the flesh': verse 3). If it comes to confidence in one's own ability to obtain salvation, Paul asserts that he was once streets ahead of anyone (verse 4). We are given here a rare insight into Paul's personal life as he shares part of his own life-story.

He reveals how his encounter with Jesus Christ on the road to Damascus (see Acts 8:1ff) shifted the grounds of his confidence for once and for all.

It is important for us to understand the authority with which Paul is writing. It is the authority of a man who knows to the very core of his being the reason for the changes that had taken place in his life.

Imagine someone running a political campaign against rich people. If such an individual was poor he could be said to be motivated by jealousy or 'having a chip on his shoulder'. But if that person came from the wealthiest of backgrounds and had voluntarily given away the last of his possessions and *chose* to become the poorest of the poor his argument would have immense moral strength. That may help us to understand the weight of Paul's words. He sets out some of his riches in the confidence market, where he was once a multi-millionaire: 'If anyone else thinks he has reason to put confidence in the flesh, I have more' (verse 4).

Paul describes the way he used to be and, in particular, the things he put his confidence in.

First, there was **his race** (verse 5): he was a Jew by birth (not conversion), a member of the tribe of Benjamin and someone who had been circumcised at the tender age of eight days, in accordance with Jewish custom based on God's instruction to Abraham (see Gn. 17:12). Paul was a thoroughbred and had once taken great pride in his background.

Then Paul was also proud of **his religion** (verse 5): he had become a Pharisee (their name meant 'The Separated Ones') whose aim in life was to seek to keep the Law of Moses even down to the smallest detail. They considered themselves as the spiritual elite and have been described as the 'spiritual athletes' of the Jewish faith. He had studied his religion under the personal tuition of a teacher called Gamaliel, the most respected Rabbi of his day (see Acts 22:3).

As well as being a member of this select group (there were no more than 6,000 of them) he distinguished himself with his commitment to the cause; 'as for zeal, persecuting the church' (verse 6). Paul had tried to stamp out every trace of those who claimed that Jesus of Nazareth was the long-awaited Jewish Messiah (see Acts 8:3). He was anxious to keep the purity of the faith of his fathers. At the time of his conversion he was on a mission to arrest believers in Damascus (see Acts 9:1ff). He had once been proud of his religious zeal.

Paul used to place confidence in **his righteousness**: '... as for legalistic righteousness, faultless' (verse 6).

The important word in this phrase is 'legalistic' (verse 6). Paul is not claiming he used to be sinless, but so far as the Pharisees' code of conduct was concerned, people would have been unable to point an accusing finger at him. He gave his energy to keeping all the rules. If there had been a 'Pharisee of the Year' award, Paul would have won it!

Before he met Jesus, Paul's 'confidence in the flesh' had been in his race, religion and righteousness. He considered that these were the qualifications that gave him standing before God. His hope of salvation was in his own hands. His credentials were impressive and fell into two categories; the first were those that were his by birth and the second category contains those that could be achieved by choice and effort.

Someone described Paul in his pre-Christian days as a man 'bleeding to climb to God'. If salvation could ever be obtained by effort, Paul had made it to the front of the queue.

Questions
1. *Are there things that you place your confidence in that are wrong?*
2. *Many people believe that salvation is obtained by virtue of things that we 'do'. How should we approach this misconception in our evangelism?*
3. *Christianity is a faith for the whole world. What does this passage teach us about our relationships to people of other faiths?*

Paul – the Christian

The 'most famous conversion in the history of the church' is how one writer has described Saul of Tarsus and his encounter with the risen Lord Jesus Christ.

Saul was a strict Pharisee and fanatically opposed to the followers of Jesus of Nazareth. On his way to Damascus where he intended to pursue disciples of Jesus his life is changed forever.

Dr Luke, who wrote the book of Acts, records the story of Saul's conversion three times (see Acts 9:1–19; 22:3–21; 26:9–17).

Paul (which was the Roman name he used and is best known by) refers to his testimony in some of his letters (see Gal. 1:11–24; 1 Tim. 1:12–16).

This autobiographical section in the letter to the Philippians (Phil. 3:4–16) is very significant as it provides an insight into Paul's attitude to his conversion not simply as an event in the past but as a continuing experience.

His encounter with the risen Lord Jesus Christ had revolutionized his life and introduced him to the Gospel of the free, forgiving love of God. That was how God had treated him – a violent persecutor of the Church! His zeal for the Jewish law had actually led him to persecute the Messiah, Jesus, so he could never trust in it again.

18

Philippians 3:7–11

The way I am now

Paul reveals how he has converted his 'profits' into 'losses'

Paul had once trusted in his race, religion and human efforts at righteousness, thinking that these things made him acceptable to God. 'But his confidence had shifted as these next few verses spell out. But whatever was to my profit I now consider loss for the sake of Christ' (verse 7). He had turned his profits to losses as a result of his encounter with the risen Jesus. His assets were now liabilities (Paul deliberately uses the language of accountancy here).

Paul has exchanged something worthless for something priceless:

> 'I consider everything a loss compared to the surpassing greatness of knowing Christ Jesus my Lord...' (verse 8)

In the past Paul had trusted in things but he now placed all his confidence in a person, the Lord Jesus Christ. This had been a costly discovery. Paul writes with feeling about having lost 'all things' for the sake of this new relationship. He had lost reputation, career, friendships and possibly family relationships. Even as he writes these words he is in prison and ultimately he will lose his life for Jesus. But when Paul considers the things he used to place his trust in he writes them off in a memorable phrase: 'I consider them rubbish, that I may gain Christ' (verse 8). He uses a word for 'dung' or 'muck' to show how worthless these things had become to him now. Paul had thrown them out in order to receive something better by far – a relationship with Jesus.

He spells out the difference this has made. He has stopped depending on 'a righteousness of my own that comes from the law (verse 9) and instead was trusting in Christ for 'a righteousness that comes from God and is by faith' (verse 9). This is called imputed righteousness which describes how God looks at us as spiritual bankrupts and credits the righteousness of Jesus to our overdrawn account.

Paul movingly continues by expressing his faith and devotion to Jesus Christ. He wants to know Jesus and to experience more of his power even though the cost in terms of suffering may well be high (verse 10). This is the language of love and provides a vivid contrast to the hard-nosed religious zealot Paul used to be.

The final verse of this section (verse 11) has caused some confusion as it seems to suggest Paul had some serious doubts about his future. He writes '... and so, somehow to attain to the resurrection from the dead' (verse 11). It may well be that Paul at times struggled with questions relating to his faith, as most Christians do. But it seems likely here, in the context of all he has been saying, that Paul is overwhelmed by the mercy of God. Out of a sense of humble appreciation he is expressing the hope 'even I, undeserving of God's kindness, will be raised with Jesus on the last day.'

Paul's conversion meant a total change of outlook. He had ceased to trust in things and now placed his confidence in a person, Jesus Christ. Notice how many times Jesus is referred to in verses 7–11; then, in contrast, look at how much of Paul's life had been self-centred (verses 4–6). This helps us to understand what conversion means. A person stops trusting in themself and puts all their faith in Jesus.

There are two further things we should note.

First, there is a popular view that 'all religions lead to God'. If this *is* true, why did God bother to save Paul? He was a zealous Jew, a deeply religious man, so why would God bother to intervene in his life? Paul's testimony demonstrates that however popular the 'all roads' view might be, it does not square with the teaching of the Bible.

Second, it has already been pointed out that salvation is seen in the New Testament in three tenses, past (I have been saved), present (I am being saved), and future (I will be saved). Paul covers all three in these verses. Some have said his personal testimony reveals the source of his theological understanding which comes through in his New Testament writings.

Paul speaks about the past (verse 9)
He speaks about the present (verse 10)
He looks to the future (verse 11)

To use the technical terms Paul deals with justification, sanctification and glorification, showing how the roots of these great themes went deep into his own experience of knowing Jesus Christ.

Questions

1. Can you think of areas of the world where Christians are facing the loss of all things for the sake of Christ? Spend some time praying for them.
2. What major changes have taken place in your life since you became a Christian? Can you identify with the things Paul used to trust in?
3. How valuable are personal stories (testimonies) in our worship and evangelism in the local church? How can they be used more effectively?

Justification by Faith

Justification is a lawyers word taken from the world of the law-courts. To justify someone is what a judge does when he finds the charge against them not proved. The accused is declared 'not guilty'

Justification by Faith (being made right with God through faith in Jesus Christ) is the central part of the Christian message. It has been described as the 'hinge of Christianity' because everything turns on it. It answers the most basic of religious questions; 'How can a man or woman be made right with God?'

The verb 'to justify' occurs thirty-nine times in the New Testament. Twenty-nine of these uses are by Paul so we realize how crucial it is to his understanding of salvation. Paul teaches that God forgives guilty people who repent (turn away) from sin and place their faith in Jesus Christ. God declares such people righteous on the basis of Grace – his love and mercy towards guilty sinners that is totally undeserved. No-one can be made right with God through their own good works. It is the sacrificial death of Jesus Christ on the cross on their behalf that is the only grounds for a person to be accepted by God (see Rom. 3:21–26; Eph. 2:8–10; Gal. 2:15–21).

Philippians 3:4–11 is an important passage of the New Testament in helping us understand how this concept of Justification by Faith alone played such an important part in Paul's life.

He had come to see all his human 'achievements' (his status as a Jew, human effort and law-keeping) as utterly useless. His only hope of being made right with a holy God was Jesus Christ. Because of Jesus, Paul had found a righteousness that did not come from keeping laws or striving to be religious – but that which is through faith in Christ – 'the righteousness that comes from God and is by faith' (Phil. 3:9). This discovery revolutionized Paul's life – and became a key element of his teaching and writing.

PRESSING ON
Philippians 3:12–4:1

19

Philippians 3:12–16

A picture of an athlete

Paul borrows a picture from the world of athletics to show the importance of moving forward in the Christian life.

Paul continues to share his personal story with the Philippians, but there is a shift in emphasis as he starts a new section of the letter which continues to 4:1. The overall theme of these verses is 'pressing on'. Paul shares his own convictions about pressing on in the Christian faith against all obstacles and opposition. He urges his fellow-believers in Philippi to have the same outlook. He concludes the section with the words: 'that is how you should stand firm in the Lord, dear friends!' (4:1). So these verses are to be seen as Paul's prescription for stable Christians. The irony is that in order to stand firm we must keep moving!

Personal example is the best teaching method in any situation, and here Paul uses it to the full. He makes several important statements about himself:

'I haven't arrived yet' (see verse 12) Paul was under no illusions about his spiritual progress – he hadn't arrived at a state of perfection with all his problems solved and questions answered. Some Christians would do well to copy his approach!

'I am not locked into the past' (see verse 13) He refers again to the Philippian believers in warm terms: 'Brothers' (verse 13). There is no sense of 'them and us' in what Paul is saying. He recognizes that his Philippian friends share in the challenge to keep pressing on. He is single-minded in his commitment to keep going forward, 'forgetting what is behind and straining towards what is ahead ...' (see verse 13). Paul is not dismissing his past as unimportant – after all he has just taken the trouble to spell out some important facts about his background. But he refuses to be caught constantly looking back to the 'golden days' when he first became a Christian.

Paul uses the picture of a runner who looks ahead to the finishing tape. Again, we can draw an important lesson from his positive outlook.

'I'm aiming to win the prize' (see verse 14) Developing his illustration from the world of athletics, Paul speaks of pressing on towards the finishing line. Refusing to look back over his shoulder, his head is down as he puts all his energy into reaching the tape. The Philippians would have easily understood his imagery as the Romans and the Greeks loved athletic competitions. The Philippians would know that often the person presiding at a contest would call the winning athlete forward to receive their prize. On occasions the winner may be summoned to the Royal Box to be honoured before the crowd. Paul views his progress as a Christian disciple in this light.

'God has called me heavenwards in Christ Jesus' (see verse 14) He writes that he has every intention of staying the course and winning the prize. Paul insists that this is not fantasy but a spiritually mature outlook (verse 15). Some in the congregation at Philippi may not fully agree with all that Paul is saying, but he is confident that God will help them understand in time (verse 15).

He concludes with a stirring challenge:

'Only let us live up to what we have already attained' (see verse 16) Once again he is pleading for the Philippians to be consistent Christians (see 1:27). Paul has no time for a standstill faith either for himself or the Philippians. Like long distance runners they are to summon every ounce of energy and keep pressing on to the finishing line.

Questions

1. Some Christians (and churches) are locked into the past. What can we learn from Paul's outlook on his personal history?

2. Can you list some of the things that distract you from running the race more effectively?

3. Is it true that some Christians give the impression that they have 'arrived'? How can we keep ourselves from falling into the trap of spiritual pride?

4. Are there specific things that God is showing your local fellowship at the moment as part of the call to press forward? Use your answers as a basis for prayer.

Winning the prize

Paul writes to the Philippians about his desire 'to win the prize' (3:14) which is a picture borrowed from the world of athletics.

Paul uses the same picture in other letters (See 1 Cor. 9:24–27; Col. 2:18; 2 Tim. 4:6–8; 2 Tim 2:5).

This image conveys several important ideas; like an athlete a Christian is called to a contest which demands single-mindedness and self-discipline. It also requires persistence and a large degree of patience.

In today's language we would talk of an athlete 'going for gold' with his or her eye on the Olympic medal.

Paul believed he was competing for a prize that God would one day give him. He wanted nothing or no-one to distract him from making the finishing line.

20

Philippians 3:17-19

A picture of an imitator

Paul tells the Philippians to imitate good examples of Christian behaviour

We have heard the saying, 'Don't do as I do – but do as I say', yet Paul is confident enough to say to the Philippians, '... join with others in following my example brothers ...' (verse 17).

Paul chooses an unusual word, linked to another word which was used to describe a performer or artist who imitates others. In today's world we would call them an impressionist or impersonator. It was not only Paul they were to copy but all those who live as consistent Christians. He instructs them to 'take note of those who live according to the pattern we gave you' (verse 17).

Paul had lived for a while with the Philippians and they had not only heard his teaching, they had seen his lifestyle. Effective discipleship involves teaching and example. The disciples asked Jesus to teach them about prayer because they saw that it played a central part in his life (Luke 11:1ff). Those of us who lead in any way need to remember that what we are and what we teach must not be separated.

Paul is not being proud in making this plea. He is simply reminding the Philippians of the importance of imitating good behaviour. (He takes the same line of approach in other letters: see Eph. 5:1; 1 Thess. 1:6; 1 Cor. 4:16.)

Paul turns to deal with bad examples, described as those who 'live as enemies of the Cross of Christ' (verse 18). He feels deeply about such people even to the point of tears. Perhaps this is because of the damage caused to young Christians or because some of the people caught up in false teaching were once close friends.

There has been much speculation about who Paul is actually speaking of in verses 18–19 – one writer lists no less than eighteen possibilities! He could be referring to a hostile anti-Christian world, or a group who were advocating a particular form of false teaching that led people into all kinds of sin. There were certain Jews who stirred up hostility against the church and Paul may be thinking of them here (see 1 Thess. 2:14–16). It is also quite possible that Paul is referring to the Judaizers whose activities he exposed a few verses earlier.

Whatever title this group went under, Paul gives a devastating assessment of them (verse 19):

'their destiny is destruction' The end of those who oppose Christ is clear, they will be destroyed. There is a sense in which this is immediately true (if you reject God's rules you reap the consequences) but it is also ultimately true. The wicked shall not inherit the Kingdom of God (1 Cor. 6:9).

'their god is their stomach' Overeating may not be the specific problem Paul is referring to here. But these are people who live for themselves and to feed their own uncontrollable appetites. They worship their appetites as if they were gods.

'their glory is in their shame' They boast about things that should really make them ashamed. They are proud of their dishonesty, immorality and godlessness. These things will one day be judged by God as sin.

'their mind is on earthly things' They are so caught up with earthly affairs they have no time for heavenly truths. They are here and now people concerned only about the material world – they are spiritually blind, deaf and dead.

Whoever 'they' are Paul is emphatic about their destiny, god, glory and mindset.

The Philippians are to take note of such bad examples and, instead, imitate the good patterns of Christian lifestyle they have seen in Paul and other believers.

Questions

1. If you were reproducing Christians like you, what shape would your local church be in?

2. If teaching and personal example go together, in what ways can we work towards producing more effective Christian disciples?

3. Consider Paul's portrait of those who live as 'enemies of the cross of Christ' (verses 18–19). Does it apply to anyone today? What should our response be to such people?

21

Philippians 3:20 – 4:1

A picture of a citizen

Paul outlines the privileges of being a citizen of heaven.

Paul introduces a concept that had meaning for the Philippian Christians, that of a citizen of a state. Philippi was proud of its status as a Roman Colony, a special honour conferred by the Emperor Octavian in 42 BC. No doubt many in the church were Roman citizens, as Paul himself was.

A Roman Colony followed Roman law, customs, language, culture and dress, even though it was on foreign soil. One writer describes a colony as 'a little piece of Rome abroad'. There was a sense of pride in being a Roman citizen: 'I may live in Philippi – but I belong to Rome' perhaps summed up how people felt about this honour.

It is against this background that Paul reminds them 'But our citizenship is in heaven' (verse 20). Paul is encouraging them to be proud of an even greater honour than being a citizen of Rome. As citizens of heaven they look forward to the coming of the King of Heaven, the Lord Jesus Christ (verse 20). Paul reminds them that when he returns the work of salvation will be completed. Our weak bodies which are subject to sin, decay and death will be changed by his power (verse 21). Paul is reminding the Philippians of the Christian hope that Jesus will one day return (see Acts 1:11; 1 Cor. 7:1 Thess. 1:10).

In using the picture of Philippi as a Roman colony Paul is reminding them of the rights and privileges of citizens of heaven. Some people may be impressed by the Emperor. Christians worship the Saviour,

Jesus. They may be awed by Rome's power – in contrast the power of Jesus 'enables him to bring everything under his control' (verse 21). Some believed that Roman influence could change the world, but citizens of Heaven looked to the day when Jesus would transform their 'lowly bodies' (verse 21). Paul wanted his friends to be proud about being Christians.

Paul concludes by reminding the Philippians he has been showing them 'how to stand firm in the Lord ...' (4:1). Perhaps here, (as in 1:27) he is putting his finger on a major problem that existed in the church. They had become discouraged and their unity was being tested. Possibly they were in danger of drifting and Paul's wise words were coming just at the right time.

Notice how warm and affectionate Paul is towards them. He uses no less than five terms of endearment in one verse, describing them as: 'my brothers'; 'beloved'; 'longed for'; 'my joy'; 'my crown', and if that is not enough he ends by calling them 'beloved' ('Dear friends!') again! This reveals something of Paul's deep affection for the church at Philippi. He is not a sergeant-major bawling at raw recruits on a parade-ground. He cares deeply for the church and has earned the right to tell them the truth (even if it hurts).

The Philippians represent the crown or wreath of victory he is competing for, they are his pride and joy. He is about to address a difficult situation and say some more uncomfortable things (verse 2ff) but it comes from the heart of a Christian leader who loves them and has their best interests in view. If we are called to lead God's people in any way, this verse makes challenging reading.

Questions

1. *Do we think enough about being citizens of heaven? What does it mean to you?*
2. *How does our heavenly citizenship relate to our earthly citizenship?*
3. *If you have any leadership responsibilities in your church, what lessons can be drawn from Paul's approach?*

HOW TO SURVIVE IN A
LOCAL CHURCH
Philippians 4:2–9

22

Philippians 4:2–3

The importance of right relationships

Paul tackles a broken relationship at Philippi

Paul knew there were a few problems in the church family at Philippi, after all, one of their leaders, Epaphroditus, was with him and undoubtedly shared news about the church. The theme of unity has been mentioned several times but now Paul addresses the matter directly. An argument has occurred between two leading members of the church which was affecting the life of the whole congregation.

The verses which deal with the problem are tantalizingly brief, leaving a wake of questions. From the information available we can work out this much:

1 An argument had arisen between two leading women in the church – *Euodia* and *Syntyche* (verse 2). It has been suggested that they were leaders in the congregation, which may or may not be the case. But they had worked together alongside Paul in the past with some degree of responsibility (verse 3).
2 The issue was threatening to split the church, although we have no indication what it was about.
3 Paul views the situation as serious and he breaks his usual pattern in similar situations, by actually naming the women.
4 Once again, we see the close relationship between Paul and the

Philippians because he felt able to address this situation with such directness.

Some Christians read the New Testament through rose-tinted glasses, believing that the first Christian congregations were a touch of heaven on earth. But when we read the letters of Paul, Peter and John carefully we begin to understand that the first Christians faced the same temptations and failures that are present in every local church in every age. The church at Philippi, despite their close relationship with the Apostle Paul, were no exception to this rule.

We know nothing more about Euodia and Syntyche outside of these verses – how sad to be remembered in such a negative way!

Every church will face disagreements and clashes of strong personalities from time to time. Paul's method of dealing with the Philippians' dilemma provides us with some helpful guidelines for surviving in a local church.

First, we notice that Paul tackles the relationship rather than the issue. He pleads with both of the women to restore the broken friendship. Paul knew what the argument was about yet he studiously avoids passing judgment as to who was right or wrong. Too often we concentrate on the issue and leave the relationship to sort itself out in time. Paul is following in a good tradition by insisting that repairing a broken friendship must take priority (see Mt. 5:23–24).

Second, Paul urges these two women to 'agree with each other in the Lord' (verse 2). That is an interesting expression. Literally Paul is asking them to '*think the same thing in the Lord*'. It is perfectly possible for Christians to agree to disagree 'in the Lord'. For example, one Christian may take the view that pacifism is right and another equally sincere believer will disagree. (Hopefully they will not come to blows about it!) They can agree that each holds thought-through beliefs and each respects the other's viewpoint. Paul is allowing the difference of *opinion* to continue – but without a break in the relationship.

This is a vital lesson if we are going to survive in a local church. Congregations have split over the most amazing issues because Christians have not learned how to deal with conflicting views.

Third, Paul appeals for others in the congregation to help. There has been some discussion as to whether Paul is appealing to an anonymous member of the church referred to as '*loyal yokefellow*' or whether he is addressing someone with the name 'Syzygus' (see NIV margin – Syzygus means 'yokefellow'). It has even been suggested Paul is appealing to the congregation as a whole to help sort the situation out. Whoever he has in mind, the point is obvious – someone needs to help Euodia and Syntyche to face up to their difficulties. When tensions and disputes arise are we known for pouring oil on the troubled waters or tipping petrol on the roaring flames? Jesus said, 'Blessed are the peacemakers for they will be called Sons of God' (Mt. 5:9).

Fourth, we note Paul's approach to a potentially explosive situation. He has acted with great sensitivity, and as a wise pastor, he has prepared the way with some good, practical teaching. (Imagine how difficult it would be for the two rival camps to sit through Philippians 2:1–11 being read without squirming!) But now, as he approaches the close of his letter, Paul has the courage and the sense of timing to tackle the problem with directness. Being a peacemaker does *not* mean ignoring important problems or brushing them under the carpet. Paul was being an effective leader and gives us all an example to follow.

Fifth, we notice that Paul saw himself as part of a team. He mentions Clement by name, alongside Euodia, Syntyche and other (anonymous) partners. Paul calls them all 'fellow workers whose names are in the book of life' (verse 3). Paul had exceptional gifts but he always seemed to work with others, suggesting that he felt this was important. In fact in the New Testament there is no support at all for the concept of a 'one-person-ministry'.

By studying Paul's method of dealing with this problem in the church at Philippi, we can learn how to handle tensions in relationships that occur in most congregations. Differences of opinion will inevitably arise – breakdowns in relationships need not!

Questions

1. *Am I better known for 'pouring oil on troubled waters' or 'pouring petrol on roaring flames'? How can I become more of a peacemaker?*

2. *As you think about your local church, are there broken relationships and unresolved issues that are being ignored? What is God telling you to do about it?*

3. *Review how Paul tackles this situation at Philippi. What have you learned from his approach?*

The Book of Life

The Book of Life is a heavenly register of those who are God's redeemed people. In secular terms it was a register of citizens (like an electoral roll). If your name was erased you were no longer a citizen.

This divine ledger is first mentioned by Moses (Ex. 32:32–33) who asks God:

> But now, please forgive their sin [the people of Israel] – but if not, then blot me out of the book you have written.

It is also mentioned in Psalm 69:28; Daniel 12:1 Philippians 4:3; and no less than six times in the book of Revelation (Rev. 3:5; 13:8; 17:8; 20:12; 20:15; 21:7). In the last of these references the context is of the 'New Jerusalem' and it reads:

> Nothing impure will ever enter it, nor will anyone who does what is shameful or deceitful, but only those whose names are written in the Lamb's book of life (Rev. 21:27).

23

Philippians 4:4–7

The importance of right reactions

Paul outlines the Christian way of reacting to problems, people and pressures

Paul passes on some valuable advice to the Philippians about facing difficult times, and through studying these verses we can discover some more survival techniques for local church life.

Paul is emphasizing the importance of right reactions when confronted with difficult problems, awkward people and daily pressures.

Reacting to problems

'Rejoice in the Lord always. I will say it again: Rejoice!' (verse 4)

The fact that Paul mentions the subject of joy so frequently in this letter (fourteen times in four chapters) suggests it was a missing note in the Philippian church at this time. Tensions in the church family, concern for Paul's welfare, the struggle of seeking to live holy lives in a hostile world had probably combined to bring a sense of spiritual flatness.

Paul gives them an important reminder ... twice over! Joy is God's gift to forgiven people (Ps. 16:11; Jn. 15:11; Rom. 14:17) and is part of the spiritual harvest the Holy Spirit produces (Gal. 5:22ff). There are times when we don't have to search for it because it fills our hearts, but what do you do when you don't *feel* joyful, and, like the Philippians, you seem surrounded by problems? Paul tells them to 'rejoice' and this is an act of the will, irrespective of whether they feel 'up or down'. He also tells them to 'rejoice in the Lord,' because he is the source of our joy and Paul believes that if the Philippians took time to reflect on his love and goodness they would have a reason to rejoice. Paul senses that some in the congregation would struggle with his advice. As if he can hear someone say 'Rejoice? You must be joking!', Paul repeats himself, 'I will say it again'. Perhaps like some in the Philippian church family the Word of God needs to be underlined for me today? It is important for us to understand that Paul is not encouraging triumphalism or a 'whistle in the dark to keep your spirits up' style of approach. He sees this as a fundamental theological principle (see 1 Thess. 5:16–18) that no matter what circumstances we face, the Christian can rejoice in the goodness of God. We may not be able to thank God *for* the problems we face but we can rejoice *in* them.

Reacting to people

Paul has already addressed the broken relationship which was affecting the whole congregation (4:2ff). It is likely that other relationships had been damaged as people had taken sides in the argument. Some were finding it difficult to get on with their fellow believers and this is not a situation unfamiliar in local churches today. Paul reveals how our reactions to people (especially awkward people!) can make all the difference. He tells them 'Let your gentleness be evident to all' (verse 5).

The word translated 'gentleness' is rich in meaning and this is seen in the variety of expressions used in different translations of the Bible; here are just a few of them:

patience, softness, modesty, a patient mind, forbearance, graciousness.

The Greeks described this characteristic as 'justice and something better than justice'. One writer describes it as 'the quality of the man who knows that rules and regulations are not the last word'. The greatest example of this stunning quality is the Lord Jesus himself and it may well be Paul is deliberately echoing the teaching he gave earlier on following Christ's example (see Phil. 2:5–11).

Paul can see that this spiritual quality was needed to heal rifts in relationships at Philippi. We need to look at our reactions to awkward people and ask God for the ability to go beyond 'doing things by the book' in order to deal with them as he deals with us – with gentleness.

Paul adds the warning 'The Lord is near' (verse 5), because all of life here and now must be viewed in the light of what will be (see I Pet. 3:1–15). How futile the Philippians' petty squabbling appears against the background of the powerful truth that Jesus Christ is coming back soon! It is a sobering thought, and one which puts some of our own disagreements into a proper perspective.

Reacting to pressures

These were anxious times for the church at Philippi. They were pre-occupied with worries about themselves, they were concerned about Paul's needs and had sent their love offering as a practical response (4:14). The various pressures had produced an anxious state of mind, which in turn was robbing them of their sense of joy. Paul gives some good advice on how to react to pressures and deal with anxiety God's way.

He begins with a firm instruction, 'Do not be anxious about anything ...' (verse 6) which is directly in line with Jesus' teaching on the same subject (Mt. 6:25). Paul deliberately makes this a command, leaving no room for anyone to duck the issue. He gives the Philippians a positive reaction to adopt when anxiety strikes ... 'but in everything, by prayer and petition, with thanksgiving, present your requests to God.' (verse 6). Notice the different words Paul uses which reveal what a rich experience prayer should be. We can pray in different ways in different places and at different times; but our prayers, petitions and requests should always be surrounded with that sense of thanksgiving.

The Philippian congregation had perhaps forgotten how important prayer was, which is a mistake more than one local church has made, to its great loss.

Paul concludes his stirring reminder about prayer with a wonderful promise. It should not be wrenched out of its context but read against the background of all that he has been saying. If we apply God's principles we can receive the gift of his peace 'which transcends all understanding' (verse 7) (we might describe it as 'beyond our capacity to understand': see Eph. 3:20). Paul speaks of this peace as a 'guard' for 'your hearts and your minds' (verse 7). He uses a vivid military term used of a detachment of soldiers who stand guard over a city and protect it from attack. (The same word is used in 2 Cor. 11:32). This strong spiritual task-force is set over the believer's *mind*, the place where anxious thoughts arise, and the *heart*, which is the control room of our innermost being.

The Philippian believers were not able to avoid pressures any more than we can. Paul tells them how to react when those pressures seem to become overwhelming – 'Don't be consumed with worry, use prayer and God will guard you from anxious thoughts.'

Is this wisdom that we need to pay attention to? (see Jas. 4:2,3). Paul is emphasizing the need for right reactions. Locked into these four verses is a storehouse of truth designed to guide the Philippians and Christian believers in other generations towards a more Christ-like lifestyle.

If you look back over these verses you will notice that Paul has emphasized four important qualities; joy, gentleness, prayerfulness and peace. And if we wish to see these qualities lived out, we could do no better than to look at the Lord Jesus himself. Perhaps this was a critical need for the Philippian church at this stage in their history, to stop looking at the problems, other people, the pressures, and model themselves instead on Jesus (2:5).

Questions

1. *Is joy a 'missing note' in your life/family/church at the present time? Can you identify the reasons why this may be the case?*

2. *Is it realistic to tell people to 'Rejoice in the Lord' when they are struggling with bereavement, serious illness, family pressures or unemployment? How do we translate this concept into our pastoral care?*

3. *Looking at your local community can you identify pressure points that affect people? What can you do as a local church to help?*

4. *How can we make prayer a richer experience for ourselves and others in our fellowship?*

The letter of joy

Paul's letter to the church in the city of Philippi has often been referred to as 'the Letter of Joy'. No less than sixteen times in four short chapters the words 'joy' or 'rejoice' occur.

What makes this more remarkable is the fact that Paul is writing from prison and facing an uncertain future. The Philippian

Christians were a great joy to Paul and he was content in the belief that God was in control of his circumstances (see 4:11).

The source of Paul's joy can be traced to his deep faith in the Lord Jesus Christ (see 3:7–11).

References to 'joy' or 'rejoicing' in Philippians

'joy'   1:4; 1:25; 2:2; 2:29; 4:1;

'rejoice'   1:18; 2:17; 2:18; 2:28; 3:1; 4:4; 4:10 (rejoice is mentioned twice in 1:18; 2:17; 2:18; and 4:4)

Why does Paul mention the subject of joy so frequently in this letter? It has been suggested that the Philippians were being robbed of this special gift that Christ gives to his followers (see Jn. 15:11).

- Some had been Christians for ten or more years and the first flush of excitement had died down.

- They were discouraged to learn of Paul's imprisonment particularly as they shared a close relationship with the apostle.

- There were internal divisions in the congregation (see 4:2) which undoubtedly caused people to take sides.

- And there were the pressures of trying to be a disciple of Jesus in a hostile, cynical world (2:15, 16).

- Paul's letter of joy came just at the right time for a congregation that needed to discover the truth that Nehemiah told the people of Israel:

  Do not grieve, for the joy of the Lord is your strength (Neh. 8:10)

24

Philippians 4:8–9

The importance of right thinking

Paul teaches that what we think affects how we behave.

Paul emphasizes in these verses how behaviour is governed by attitudes. The challenge to the Philippian church was, 'think about the way you think!'

Paul repeats his 'Finally my brothers' of 3:1 and prepares to draw his letter to a close. He urges the congregation with some words which were possibly familiar. It has been suggested that Paul is quoting from a manual on popular moral teaching from a non-Christian source. If this is the case, he could be making an important point that not everything about human culture is bad. Non-Christians can often analyze what is missing, it is finding *what* is missing that proves a more complex problem! Whether the words are original to Paul or borrowed from elsewhere, through the inspiration and intervention of the Holy Spirit, we find them in our Bible. Paul urges his Philippian friends to fill their minds with (verse 8):

'whatever is true' as opposed to things that are false and deceitful.

'whatever is noble' in contrast to things that are dishonourable or unworthy.

'whatever is right' as against things that are wrong.

'whatever is pure'   in contrast to things that are dirty.

'whatever is lovely'   as opposed to things that are morally ugly.

'whatever is admirable'   rather than things that are disreputable.

'whatever is excellent'   in contrast to things that are shoddy.

'... or praiseworthy'   as against things that are shameful.

Like a single diamond with many facets, Paul sketches out the thinking pattern of a man or woman who wants to be holy.

It is possible that the Philippian believers had become negative in their outlook. They had allowed their minds to be filled with unhelpful thoughts. This was spilling over into other areas of their lives. Paul's instructions were designed to get their minds feeding on good things. It has been said, 'a man is not what he thinks he is, but what he *thinks* he *is*'. Changed thinking habits eventually produce changed behaviour patterns.

Paul then makes a startling comment; 'whatever you have learned or received or heard from me or seen in me – put it into practice.' (verse 9) Paul's relationship and testimony with the Philippians was such that he does not just remind them of his sermons, he can point them to his lifestyle! He had lived with the Philippian believers, they had heard him preach publicly and explain Christian truth privately. They had seen that the truth worked out in his own life and it was this example Paul was urging them to copy. This presents a powerful challenge to any who aspire to be leaders in God's church, (see Js. 3:1,2). People need to see what we are, not just listen to what we say. Paul concludes with a promise, 'And the God of peace will be with you ...' (verse 9). Earlier he has written about 'the peace of God' (verse 7) as a guard for anxious minds and troubled hearts. Now it is the God who is the source of all peace that Paul refers to. 'The peace of God' is based on the promise of his protection and the phrase 'the God of peace' is a reminder of the promise of his presence.

In this section (verses 2–9) Paul has touched on 'nitty-gritty' issues concerning life in a local church. He has emphasized some survival principles that we can adopt. Hopefully they will help us do more than just survive in our local church – but to actually enjoy being part of it and to make a full contribution to its growth and development. Like the Philippian congregation, we need to cultivate right relationships, right reactions and right thinking if we are to achieve this goal.

Questions

1. *Computer programmers tell us 'Garbage in = Garbage out'. How can we cultivate the skill of right thinking?*
2. *Paul places great emphasis on teaching and personal example. How can we practically bring these things more closely together in local church life?*
3. *Are there some things in your culture which can be 'borrowed' and used to teach Christian values?*
4. *Review the 'survival principles' of verses 2–9. Do some have particular relevance for your church at this time?*

The mind

Paul tells the Philippians that filling their minds with good things is important. The importance of the mind is stressed in other parts of the Bible. For example:

The **'sinful mind'** is hostile to God. But the **'mind controlled by the Spirit'** leads to life and peace. (Romans 8:5–8)

Changed behaviour is directly linked to **'the renewing of your mind'**. (Romans 12:1–2)

People who live unholy lives are described as being **'darkened in their understanding'**. (Ephesians 4:17–19)

Jesus declares that the greatest commandment is to **'Love the Lord your God with all your heart and with all your soul and with all your mind'**. (Matthew 22:37)

Paul speaking about praying and singing **'with my spirit ... also ... with my mind'**. (1 Corinthians 14:15–19)

God has given us minds to think with. Our minds help us to grasp truth and we can use them to discover the liberating gospel (Jn. 8:32) and to offer our worship to God (Jn. 4:23).

We must guard against two opposite extremes. One is *anti-intellectualism* when the place of careful thinking, study and research is rejected. The other is *arid intellectualism* where theology is divorced from practical Christian living and becomes the preserve of a small and obscure group of academics. God has given us our minds as a gift and we are to use them for his glory.

CARING AND SHARING
Philippians 4:10–23

25

Philippians 4:10–13

The secret of happiness

Paul reveals how he can face any situation in life through Christ's strength.

Paul now turns to the main reason for writing his letter to the Philippians – to say 'thank you' for the gift they had sent him with Epaphroditus. He is grateful for their kindness which prompts him to 'rejoice greatly in the Lord' (verse 10) and he expresses his thanks for their gift with great sensitivity – there is no hint that he is asking for more! Paul acknowledges that their care comes from a personal concern the Philippians have had for a long time (verse 10). They had wanted to make a gift in support of Paul's ministry earlier, but for various reasons it had not been possible.

Paul shares that, at the current time, he has no pressing financial problems. He tells his Philippian friends, 'I have learned to be content whatever the circumstances' (verse 11). He goes on to explain that he has 'learned the secret of being content in any and every situation,' (verse 12).

He deliberately chooses a word for 'secret' which means 'to be initiated' (it is used of a person entering into a mystery religion through a secret rite) which suggests this is something profound that has been revealed to him over a period of time. He has discovered the secret of true happiness. There have been occasions in his ministry when he has been well looked after to the extent that he has had more than enough: 'plenty ... well fed' (verse 12). Equally there have been time of great personal hardship when he has gone without: 'in ... need ... hungry ...

in want' (verse 12). When we examine carefully the record of Paul's ministry it bears out what he is saying here (see 2 Cor. 11:23–29). He faced a wide range of difficult situations which could easily have bred deep insecurity in Paul. Perhaps at times this was a spiritual battle he had to face, but his testimony to the Philippian church is that he has learned the secret of deep-down contentment, no matter what situation he found himself in. What was Paul's secret discovery? He reveals it in the very next phrase: 'I can do everything through him who gives me strength' (verse 13).

He had discovered that there was not a single situation he was called to face where Jesus was not with him. Paul is not suggesting he is a Christian version of Superman, for whom nothing is impossible. Rather, he can cope with anything because the Lord gives him the strength he needs. Paul was able to write about the 'peace of God which transcends all understanding' (verse 7) because he had experienced it countless times – and still could not understand it!

There were occasions when he had been at ease when it was illogical to feel that way. Eleven or so years previously in the city of Philippi he had sat in a jail cell battered and bleeding and discovered the strength to sing worship songs (see Acts 16:25).

Paul was one of the most robust Christians that has ever lived and he faced incredible difficulties during his ministry. But his toughness was not a product of human skill – according to Paul it was the strength of Christ at work in his life. In case the Philippians – or any other Christians – would want to place Paul on a pedestal as a megastar disciple he gives his secret away: 'It isn't me, it is Jesus *in* me!' Of course Paul had to do his part in terms of obedience, faith and commitment – there was perspiration as well as inspiration! He is telling the Philippians this open secret that the strength that Christ gives is sufficient for anything we face in life. Paul's discovery was, no doubt, a great encouragement to the church in Philippi, particularly to those who had felt like giving up. But these verses also help us to nail a couple of myths in our modern world.

Myth 1 teaches: 'Things make you happy'. But this is untrue as a glimpse beneath the surface of this superficial statement will show. A person can collect all the things they have ever wanted and still feel desperately empty. Paul discovered the secret of happiness was not things, but a relationship with Jesus Christ. His own testimony was that he had lost 'things' in order to find Christ (see Phil. 3:8).

Myth 2 says: 'All you need is within yourself'. This century the Western world has made self-centredness a boom industry. Self-awareness, self-expression, self-realization and more beside have been the subject of books, seminars and videos in many countries. Paul was no stranger to such ideas. His use of the word translated '*content*' (NIV) is a deliberate choice. Some philosophers of his day used this very word to teach self-sufficiency and claimed it was the highest goal a person could reach. People, things, relationships, ceased to have any hold. Through the pathway of the mind an individual could reach this inner state of contentment and self-sufficiency.

But Paul is clear in his argument. He is not self-sufficient but Christ-sufficient. He had learned a secret that he was keen to pass on. No matter what challenges lay ahead, Jesus Christ was big enough to meet them with him, through him, in him and for him. As the Philippian believers would have well understood, even as Paul wrote these words he was being called to live them out in his current, very uncertain situation.

Questions

1. *How does your church handle the subject of money, in particular financial giving? What light does this passage throw on the subject?*
2. *Paul knew what it was to be hungry, in need and in want. Are there situations in the world where this is true for certain groups of people? What is God saying to you about this?*
3. *Look at the two modern myths that are exposed by Paul's teaching. Are there others you can think of that need to be countered?*
4. *Are you on the way to discovering Paul's secret of 'contentment'? Can you identify some of the obstacles?*

26

Philippians 4:14–20

The joy of giving

Paul shows how giving affects others, the givers and God.

For some Christians the subject of giving is anything but joyful, maybe because they have never understood what real Christian giving is, and why it is so important. As well as expressing his thanks to the Philippians for the love-gift, Paul reveals three important truths about giving.

Giving affects others

Paul is grateful to the Philippians for their willingness to stand with him in practical support (verse 14). Their love-gift was not a 'one-off' gesture, they had supported Paul consistently from their earliest days as Christians. When Paul had left their region (Macedonia) no other church supported his ministry financially except the congregation at Philippi (verse 15). It has been suggested that Paul would not accept financial help from any church other than Philippi which would indicate one reason for his special relationship with them. Their giving had been consistent and they had remained sensitive and responsive to Paul's needs (verse 16).

The picture we get is of a caring and sharing church – which stands in contrast to some of the frank things Paul has said elsewhere in this letter. Their giving had made a deep impact on Paul. He knew that behind the monetary gifts there were people who were deeply committed to him as a friend. His words at the start of this letter (1:3–5) sum up the way in which their practical partnership had touched him. In spite of the warning against self-centredness (2:4) the Philippians had an enviable track record in caring for Paul.

Giving affects the givers

Paul borrows the language of the business world as he writes of the spiritual blessings that will result from the Philippians' generosity. He is not so much concerned about receiving their gift as the 'spiritual interest' that will be 'credited to your account' (verse 17). Paul has already referred to giving as a two way process 'the matter of giving and receiving ...' (verse 15) because he knows that when a gift is given the one who receives *and* the one who gives are both affected as a direct result.

Paul sees their systematic, faithful, compassionate giving as an indicator of their spiritual health. He teaches elsewhere that giving (or the lack of it) has a direct bearing on spiritual growth (see 2 Cor. 9:6; Gal. 6:7–10). The Lord Jesus taught about the importance of storing up 'treasures in heaven' rather than on earth (Mt. 6:19–24) and that 'it is more blessed to give than to receive' (Acts 20:35). The Philippians had no doubt discovered that this was true.

Paul is not looking for more money – the gifts they have sent with Epaphroditus have left him 'amply supplied' (verse 18) – he is more concerned with the spiritual growth that follows on from the act of giving.

Giving affects God

Paul switches from the language of the city to use the vocabulary of the temple. The Philippians' gifts to Paul are seen by God and are described as 'a fragrant offering' (like incense burnt on the altar), 'an acceptable sacrifice' (like an animal brought as a sacrificial gift) 'pleasing to God' (verse 18). The lesson is clear, God is affected by our giving. This is the reason that some churches today insist on calling the collection of money during the service, '*the offering*'. That is what it is, an offering of gifts to God as an expression of our love for him.

Paul knew that the Philippians' gifts to him had not gone unrecorded in the ledgers of Heaven, and he wanted them to know that too.

He concludes his '*thank you*' section with what some consider to be a promise and others a prayer-wish:

> 'And my God will meet all your needs according to his glorious riches in Christ Jesus' (verse 19).

In either case it contains the profound thought that just as the Philippians have been concerned to meet Paul's needs, God will meet theirs too. There are two important qualifications:

1 God will meet their *needs* rather than their *wants* – there is often a significant difference between the two!

2 God will meet these needs according to his riches *not* out of his riches. A millionaire may donate £1,000 to a charity out of his riches – but compared to his total wealth it is a small amount. But if he gave according to his riches it would be significantly larger. God's giving is in proportion to his infinite resources – described by Paul as 'according to his glorious riches in Christ Jesus' (verse 19).

Paul concludes this thank you with an expression of praise to God which is hardly surprising in the light of all he has just shared. God who is 'Father' to Paul, the Philippian church and to followers of Jesus in every age, deserves praise and glory for ever (verse 20). Such doxologies as they are called are not unfamiliar in Paul's letters (see Gal. 1:5; 1 Tim. 6:16; 2 Tim. 4:18 etc.). But they do represent more than a formal end to a letter. They come from the heart of a man who is deeply aware of the grace of God.

Paul's thoughts on the subject of giving deserve careful thought. Although in this context the gifts Paul received from the Philippians would probably have been mainly financial, giving is a much broader issue. Giving obviously involves our money, but also included are things such as friendship, hospitality, time, encouragement, prayer, a willingness to meet practical needs ... the list is a long one. Do we need to develop 'the grace of giving'? (See 2 Cor. 8:7.)

Questions

1. 'Giving Christians grow and growing Christians give'. Is this true in your experience?

2. How openly is the subject of giving discussed in your local church? Are there specific ways this could be encouraged more?

3. How faithful are we in long-term giving compared to the Philippians' continued support for Paul?

4. When you look at the world church, how does your national church rate in terms of generosity?

5. Think of some people in your circle of influence who need some form of gift today.

Giving

Financial giving is dealt with openly in the New Testament. Paul gives the Corinthian Church two whole chapters of important teaching on the subject (see 2 Cor. 8–9).

The first Christians in Jerusalem shared their money with others in need (Acts 2:45). There is no suggestion that this was compulsory. It seems to have been a spontaneous act that was one of the tangible results of the Holy Spirit being poured out on them at Pentecost.

The new believers in Antioch responded to news of an impending famine by sending a love-gift of money to Jerusalem (Acts 11:27–30).

Paul instructs Timothy that good leaders should be paid well (see 1 Tim. 5:17–18) and also warns that love of money is a root of all kinds of evil (1 Tim. 6:10).

27

Philippians 4:21–23

Paul's goodbye

Paul signs off in a way that tells of the grace and power of the Lord Jesus Christ.

Paul has reached the end of his letter. It is likely that the bulk of it has been dictated by him personally and faithfully written down by one of his helpers. But Paul (in common with the customs of the day) would probably write the last few sentences in his own hand concluding with his signature that showed the letter was not a forgery (see 1 Cor. 16:21; Gal. 6:11; 2 Thess. 3:17).

Paul's final greetings give some interesting insights. First, Paul writes 'Greet all the saints in Christ Jesus' (verse 21: literally, 'greet every saint'). Paul intends that no one individual should be singled out or missed out. He usually ends his letters with a list of personal greetings to various people (see Rom. 16:3ff!) but on this occasion he gives no-one special mention in spite of his close ties with the church. This may have been because Epaphroditus (who would have carried the letter to Philippi 'by hand') had been given a long list of personal messages or possibly Paul felt that to single out some for special mention would have gone against the spirit of his teaching on humility! But we are reminded that churches are *people*, not buildings, and people who are individuals, each one special to God.

Second, we notice that Paul is not alone. He mentions 'The brothers who are with me send greetings' (verse 21). Paul was under arrest but had enjoyed certain privileges (see Acts 28:30–31). Timothy and Epaphroditus were with him and possibly Dr Luke (who wrote Acts as well as the Gospel of Luke) was there too.

Often in the darkest times God puts someone alongside us as an encourager. Thank God for such friendships! It is important to keep our eyes open for those who may need someone to come alongside and help them through a tough patch. Such sensitivity is a mark of a church that cares and shares.

Third, Paul makes a startling statement in what is almost a throw-away line: 'All the saints send you their greetings; especially those who belong to Caesar's household' (verse 22). In passing on the greetings of the believers in Rome he mentions that some of them are members of the Imperial Household. This does not mean they were in Caesar's immediate family circle, but rather they were members of his staff. These may have been slaves or soldiers that had come to personal faith in Jesus. The significant fact to note is that within approximately thirty years of the crucifixion of Jesus, the message of the gospel had penetrated to the very centre of the Roman Empire. Paul has already mentioned that the palace guard had come into contact with the Christian message (1:13) and now he refers to members of Caesar's staff who were believers.

We must never place limits on the Holy Spirit's ability to work. He is, thankfully, not limited to operating within the bounds of our endeavours. He is *God the evangelist* seeking to draw people of every race and background to personal faith in Jesus Christ.

Finally, we notice that Paul concludes with a benediction (or blessing) 'The grace of the Lord Jesus Christ be with your spirit. Amen' (verse 23).

It is appropriate that Paul's final words to his Philippian friends should be about Jesus. Paul has made it plain that there is no-one like Jesus (1:12; 3:10) and the greatest gift he can send his friends is the prayer that the grace of the Lord Jesus that has transformed Paul, may be poured out on their lives as well.

Questions

1. *If it is true that 'the church is people not buildings' how should it affect our priorities?*

2. *Are there people that you know (Christian or non-Christian) who need an encourager to come alongside them at the moment?*

3. *Do we limit God in our evangelism? Start to pray for some 'impossible' people to come to personal faith in Jesus.*

4. *What are the main themes of Paul's letter? How many of them relate to you and your church in a particular way at the moment?*

Did Paul visit Philippi again?

The answer to this question is that we cannot be certain that he did. Our last glimpse of Paul in Acts 28:30–31 has left many unanswered questions. Some believe he was tried before Caesar, sentenced to death and executed. But, if this is the case, we are left wondering why Dr Luke makes no mention of Paul's death in Acts.

Others hold the view that Paul was released having won his case only to be arrested again during Emperor Nero's reign. Nero made the Christians scapegoats for the great Fire of Rome (AD 64) and terrible persecutions followed. Those who hold this view claim Paul was martyred somewhere between AD 65–68.

If this is correct, it is quite possible that Paul would have made a return visit to his friends in Philippi.

For further reading

A large number of commentaries have been written on Philippians over the years. Out of a long list of titles, three have been selected as being suitable for the readers of the Crossway Bible Guide series.

William Hendriksen, *Philippians: New Testament Commentary* (Banner of Truth Trust, London, 1962).

Ralph P Martin, *Philippians: Tyndale New Testament Commentary* (Inter-Varsity Press, London, 1959).

Alec Motyer *The Message of Philippians: Bible Speaks Today* (Inter-Varsity Press, Leicester, 1984).

PROPHET
A NOVEL
Frank E. Peretti

' *You will know the truth, and the truth will set you free*' (John 8: 32)

John Barrett, anchorman for 'NewsSix at Five', the city's most watched newscast, has a problem. His comfortable, successful world is being jarred to breaking point. He's caught his producer skewing a story to fit her own prejudices, then lying to cover her tracks – and she appears to be hiding something much bigger. His father's 'accidental' death suddenly isn't looking so accidental. Carl, his estranged son, has returned to challenge his integrity and probe to find the man behind the TV image. The supposedly professional and objective newsroom is now divided and fighting over Truth. And what are these mysterious 'voices' Barrett is hearing ...?

Once again, master storyteller **Frank Peretti** has woven a prophetic tale for our times. *Prophet* carries all the hallmarks of Frank's blockbusting fiction – plenty of edge-of-the-seat action, nail-biting suspense, breakneck pacing, and blow-you-out-of-the-water spiritual impact. But more than this, it penetrates to the very heart of a vast struggle that threatens to tear our society to pieces, the struggle over which vision of moral authority will define our nation.

THE CHURCH THAT TURNED THE WORLD UPSIDE DOWN

Roy Clements

So great an impact did the early Christians make on those around them that people said that they had turned the world upside down.

We too should make the same impression, at home, at work, at leisure. We often feel intimidated by the task, so how much more should the early church have had cause to be frightened – a tiny band of believers in a hostile world. Yet within a few years the church had grown to thousands across the Roman empire.

The lessons they learned are as applicable today as ever. In this masterful study of Acts, Roy Clements shows us how we too can turn the world upside down.

Roy Clements is the Pastor of Eden Chapel in Cambridge. Well known as a speaker at many events, he is also the author of several books. He is married to Jane, with three children.

A PASSION FOR HOLINESS
J. I. Packer

Changing our lives for the better

The sequel to *Keep in Step with the Spirit*.

'This will take our best thinking and our most faithful living.'

Richard Foster

'No one is better qualified to address this call.'

Chuck Colson

As Christians succumb more and more to materialism, holiness is becoming the forgotten virtue of the Church. Yet, as the Bible makes clear, holiness is high on God's priorities for his people.

J. I. Packer brings us back to where God wants us to be. He shows us that holiness is nothing less than a lifelong passion for loving God and following his ways.

J. I. Packer is Professor of Systematic and Historical Theology at Regent College, Vancouver, Canada, and has also held posts in his native Britain. Dr. Packer is the author of numerous best-sellers including *Knowing God, Keep in Step with the Spirit* and most recently *Among God's Giants*.

MY PATH OF PRAYER
Edited by David Hanes

Personal experiences of God

David Watson, J. I. Packer, Derick Bingham, Michael Baughen, Edward England, Jean Darnall, J. Oswald Sanders, Selwyn Hughes, Phyllis Thompson, Jean Wilson, Richard Wurmbrand.

'Unusually helpful contribution to the needs of ordinary battle-scarred Christians.'

Michael Green

Here is a book that will encourage us to pray, based on the personal experiences of some leading Christians. By discovering the secrets of their prayer lives we learn to approach our Heavenly Father more easily ourselves.

This classic book, now reissued, will speak to you today.

SWEET AND SOUR PORK
THE JOYS AND PAINS OF A PRODIGAL SON
Jeff Lucas

With honesty and lots of humour, Jeff Lucas offers us answers to some down to earth questions.

- Can we find contentment in life?
- What is repentance all about?
- Why do I still feel guilty when I know that God has forgiven me?
- Is it fun being a Christian?

Discover how Father God has invited each one of us to a very special celebration.

'This is my kind of book. It has that very rare quality of being profoundly biblical, at the same time as being extremely readable, down to earth and practical. I can honestly say that my only regret is that it wasn't written 20 years ago when I was first a Christian. It is witty, enlightening, compassionate and deeply challenging. If you're anything like me, *Sweet and Sour Pork* will make you laugh, make you think and help you to see both God and yourself that much more clearly.'

Steve Chalke

'This book deals a major blow to the sort of Christianity which has little to do with Christ. It is a must for those who feel they have failed and can't start again, have sinned and can't find a way back, have lost faith and are unsure of the Father's welcome.'

Gerald Coates

Jeff Lucas is a regular Spring Harvest speaker with an international teaching ministry. He and his family live in Chichester, where he works with Revelation Church and the Pioneer Team.

THE DILEMMA OF SELF-ESTEEM
Alister and Joanna McGrath

Low self-esteem can be a crippler. It can hinder people from achieving their potential. It can sabotage relationships and careers. It can keep even the most dedicated Christians from fulfilling God's purpose for their lives.

Yet so many who promote positive self-esteem have ignored the reality of sin and the need for humility. Often the price paid for positive self-esteem is a dilution of the gospel. So how should Christians deal with the problem of a negative self-image?

The path to the answer leads through some intriguing terrain. Human infants in all cultures follow a basic, primal instinct to attach emotionally to parents (or another close adult). Given a choice, infants often prefer love to food. Even higher forms of animal life exhibit attachment behaviour. But a separation of mother and infant (perceived by the child as abandonment) may disturb this attachment, damaging the child's self-esteem. So for the Christian, once separated from God by sin, self-worth and acceptance are grounded in an attachment to God through Christ.

In this important book, the McGraths take the best of recent psychological research and set it alongside a responsible Biblical approach to the subject. They point out the valid insights of modern psychology,, but at the same time, they deal with the tensions between the gospel and most secular psychotherapies. Here is an in-depth, sensitive analysis of a crucial subject for the church.

Joanna McGrath is principal clinical psychologist at the Rivermead Rehabilitation Unit in Oxford, England.

Alister McGrath, author of many books and frequent conference speaker, teaches theology at Wycliffe Hall, Oxford University.

HEALING LIFE'S HIDDEN ADDICTIONS
Dr. Archibald Hart

Self-Hatred ● *Worry* ● *Entertainment* ● *Food* ● *Sex* ● *Shopping*
Work ● *Codependency* ● *Control* ● *Exercise*

So, you don't take drugs, you don't have a drink problem, you gave up smoking years ago. So, you don't have to worry about addictions?

In *Healing Life's Hidden Addictions*, Dr Hart explores fascinating new research which shows that our inner compulsions are addictive, and not only do they waste much of our time, but they also control our lives.

In addition to offering sound medical and psychological insight, Hart probes deeply into the spiritual dynamics of addiction and points the way for release from them.

'I think it is quite brilliant. I found the book professional, very interesting, informative, thorough, with clear definitions and helpful conclusions. There is a good balance between the physical, psychological and spiritual.'

Helena Wilkinson, author and lecturer for CWR, and editor of
The Christian Counsellor

Dr Archibald Hart is a prolific author and Dean in a school of psychology researching the most effective ways of overcoming addictive behaviours.